WEST SUSSEX CHURCH WALKS

40 Walks to 100 Churches

Diana Pé

Published by Sigma Leisure – an imprint of
Sigma Press, 1 South Oak Lane, Wilmslow, Cheshire SK9 6AR, England.

British Library Cataloguing in Publication Data
A CIP record for this book is available from the British Library.

ISBN: 1-85058-659-4

Typesetting and Design by: Sigma Press, Wilmslow, Cheshire.

Cover: Audrey Stephens

Illustrations: Doreen Peskett

Photographs: Diana Pé and Doreen Peskett

Maps: Jeremy Semmens

Printed by: MFP Design and Print

Disclaimer: the information in this book is given in good faith and is believed to be correct at the time of publication. No responsibility is accepted by either the author or publisher for errors or omissions, or for any loss or injury howsoever caused. Only you can judge your own fitness, competence and experience.

Preface

All the walks described in this book, apart from the last two, can be found in Ordnance Survey Landranger Map 197. Walks 39 and 40 are on OS Landranger 198. The new Explorer Maps are clearer and more detailed. At the start of each walk is a reference to the relevant Explorer Map. It is a good idea to bring this map on your walks, even though we have drawn diagrams and given written directions. The diagrams are not to scale and rarely show hills, woodland or small streams.

The inspiration for this book has been my delight in rambling in the Downs and seeing in the distance, above a quiet hamlet, the tower of an unpretentious church. Our minds go back to the shepherds, pedlars and other travellers who came down this same flint track and sought refuge in this same flint church, back in centuries we can hardly imagine. For them it was a haven from the storm as well as a holy place. For them, emerging from their hovels a thousand years ago, this building must have seemed magnificent. For us, a thousand years later its beauty is its ancient simplicity. It has become a double haven: from foul weather and from foul 20th-century fumes and frenetic lifestyles. Beautiful villages, soft hills and warm woods enfold these precious churches still.

Now, at the end of the 20th century, many village churches are still unlocked. If they are locked, sadly this is a measure to keep out vandals. It is usually possible to shelter in the porch and find the key from a neighbour. **Please cover your boots before entering a church** (plastic bags and elastic bands are useful for this purpose).

Acknowledgements

I should like to record my gratitude to the following for their help in the preparation of this book: John Avenell, Gabrielle Ma, Tony Pé, Robert Pé, Esmond Pope, Kathleen Ramsay, Jim Smith and Peggy Synge.

Rights of Way on the Sussex Downs

New public rights of way posts have been appearing all over the Downs in the past few years. The Susses Downs Conservation Board has introduced the National colour coding system which includes coloured arrows indicating the status of the path, as follows:
Yellow = Public Footpath; Blue= Public Bridleway; Red = Byway; Green = Roads used as Public Paths.

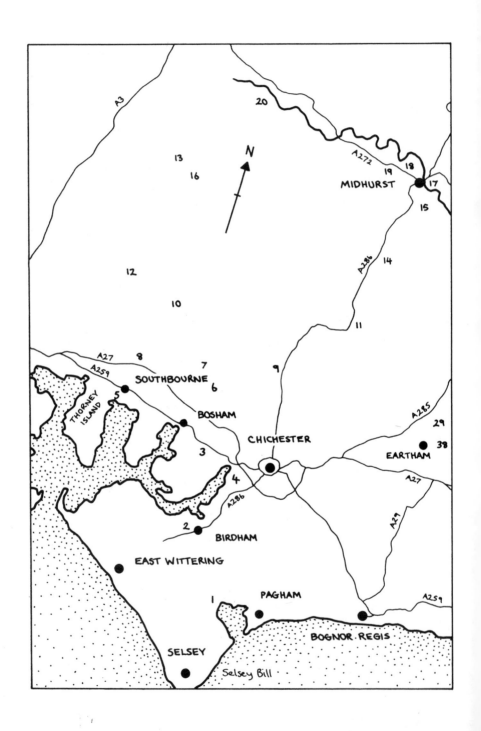

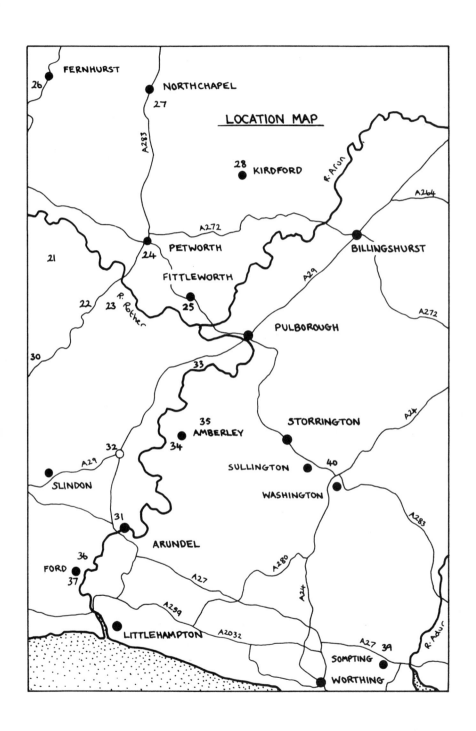

LOCATION MAP

Contents

An Introduction to Medieval Churches in Sussex   1

Features of Medieval Church Architecture   4

10 Walks near Chichester

Walk 1: Pagham Harbour, Church Norton and Sidlesham   8
Distance: 3 miles or 7 miles

Walk 2: Birdham, Itchenor and West Wittering   11
Distance: 8 to 9 miles

Walk 3: Chichester, Bosham and Fishbourne   15
Distance: 5 to 6 miles

Walk 4: Fishbourne and Apuldram   19
Distance: 3 to 4 miles

Walk 5: Prinsted, Chidham and Southbourne   22
Distance: 5 miles, with an optional 3-mile extension

Walk 6: Sennicotts, Funtington and West Stoke   26
Distance: 6 to 7 miles

Walk 7: West Stoke, Kingley Vale and Stoughton   30
Distance: 7 miles

Walk 8: Racton, Stansted House and Chapel   34
Distance: 5 miles

Walk 9: Binderton, The Trundle and Lavant   38
Distance: 5½ miles

Walk 10: Stoughton Down, Up Marden, North Marden and East Marden   41
Distance: 7 miles

10 Walks near Midhurst

Walk 11: Singleton, West Dean and the Trundle   46
Distance: 6 miles

Walk 12: Compton, Chalton and Idsworth   49
Distance: 8 miles

Walk 13: South Harting and Buriton   53
Distance: 8½ miles

Walk 14: Cocking and Heyshott   57
Distance: 5 miles

Walk 15: West Lavington and Bepton   61
Distance: 9 miles

Walk 16: Harting Down, Didling and Elsted   65
*Distance: 8 to 9 miles for the longer route **or** 5 to 6 miles.*

Walk 17: Midhurst, Lodsworth and Easebourne   69
Distance: 9 miles

Walk 18: Stedham, Iping and Woolbeding   73
Distance: 8 miles

Walk 19: Dumpford, Chithurst and Trotton   77
Distance: 3 to 4 miles

Walk 20: Habin Bridge, Terwick and Rogate   81
Distance: 5 miles

10 Walks near Petworth

Walk 21: Graffham and Selham   86
Distance: 6 to 7 miles

Walk 22: Duncton, Burton Park and Seaford College   90
Distance: 6 to 7 miles

Walk 23: Burton Park, Barlavington, Sutton and Coates   94
Distance: 6 miles or 8 miles

Walk 24: Petworth, Upperton and Tillington   98
Distance: 4 to 5 miles

Walk 25: Fittleworth, Egdean and Stopham   103
Distance: 8 miles

Walk 26: Fernhurst and Lurgashall   108
Distance: 7 or 8 miles

Walk 27: Northchapel, Ebernoe and Ebernoe Common   112
Distance: 5 to 6 miles

Walk 28: Kirdford and Wisborough Green   116
Distance: 8 miles

Walk 29: Eartham and Boxgrove   119
Distance: 6 miles

Walk 30: Upwaltham, East Dean and the South Downs Way   123
Distance: 8 miles

10 Walks near Arundel

Walk 31: Arundel, South Stoke, North Stoke and Burpham   128

Distance: 10 miles

Walk 32: Whiteways, Bury and Bignor   133

Distance: 8 to 9 miles

Walk 33: Greatham Bridge, Hardham, Coldwaltham and Watersfield   137

Distance: 7 miles

Walk 34: Amberley, The Wild Brooks and Greatham   141

Distance: 6 miles

Walk 35: Rackham, Parham and Wiggonholt   144

Distance: 6 to 7 miles

Walk 36: Tortington and Binsted   148

Distance: 5 to 6 miles

Walk 37: Ford, Climping and Yapton   152

Distance: 7 miles (with optional 4 miles)

Walk 38: Eartham, Slindon and Madehurst   156

Distance: 4 miles or 11 miles

Walk 39: Sompting and Coombes   161

Distance: 7 miles

Walk 40: Washington Common, Sullington and Washington   165

Distance: 5 to 6 miles

Bibliography   **168**

An Introduction to Medieval Churches in Sussex

The Parish Church at Norton

Building churches was a favoured pastime of Saxon villagers. They put their souls into the churches and the buildings communicate with us. They tell us of the skills, beliefs and deep religious fervour of a people who lived one thousand years ago. In some cases their villages have vanished and only a lone church stands to bear witness to its existence. The church may be battered and restored, it may reflect the sophisti-cated devices of succeeding generations but its Saxon soul is still there in the chancel arch or the lintel or stone font. We, a deeply materialistic people, may not appreciate the spiritual impact of Christianity on seventh-century England. Kings, leaders and priests gave up earthly ambitions and devoted themselves to prayer, teaching and pilgrimage. Wilfrid was one Christian leader who, with his followers in Selsey, con-verted the south Saxons. His religious community in Selsey, formed in

AD681, was the first cathedral in Sussex. Small parishes grew up even in remote places. The first churches were wooden with thatched roofs. They were liable to be burnt by invading Danes. Saxons developed skills of stone building, stone and wood carving, plastering and painting. Saxon churches were small, individual buildings made with local stones, downland flint and brick Roman remains. Pulborough sandstone was difficult to cut without causing it to crumble so large slabs were used. The Saxon church consists of two parts. First, the smaller, more sacred chancel stands to the east, and usually has a square end. Here the leader, later known as 'Parson' conducted service from the altar. The chancel is linked by a curved arch to the larger nave. The congregation stood here throughout the service on an earth floor which was strewn with rushes. Only the old and weak could sit on the stone bench beside the walls of the nave. The nave was also used for meetings, sometimes even markets and plays.

Saxon villages were small, some under 10 households. One of the villagers who toiled in the field was parson or chief man. He took mass and had powers to excommunicate, a terrible punishment then. The sinners were buried outside the churchyard or God's Acre. The virtuous were usually buried inside the church itself. After service there might be dancing, ball games or archery outside. Yew trees were planted and provided bows for archers.

Some of the churches were crowned with towers and, as by a miracle, some of the towers still stand today. Singleton Church has a low, square, solid tower. Sompting has a tall, slender tower with four-sided gabled spire, the only example standing in England. Bosham tower is neat with a shapely steeple. All these towers are on the west side, and in the case of Bosham it serves as a guide to sailors in the harbour.

Arches, doorways and window openings were usually rounded; a few were triangle-headed. 'Long and short work' was with stones set alternately horizontally and vertically. The tower arch of Bosham Church is one example of this Saxon building art.

Norman influence was felt in Sussex even before the Conquest. Norman styles and materials crossed the Channel. Stone from Caen was a precious, more malleable building material. Norman mouldings of zigzag or chevron were reproduced and developed with imaginative improvisation, as on the doorway of Climping tower. The Normans established the curved or apsidal east end as standard. Both North Marden and Upwaltham Churches have apsidal chancels.

For some reason the Normans were keen to live in Sussex. William

The Conqueror was determined to impose his authority. The cathedral was moved from Selsey to Chichester and the new building was large and impressive. The nave and transepts of the cathedral and the nave of Amberley are early Norman. As a cathedral city, Chichester's population grew and it became an administrative centre. Many more monasteries and priories were founded under the Normans. Rules were stricter than in Saxon times. The Church preached the duties of submission and loyalty. Masons were kept busy enlarging and rebuilding Saxon churches.

A century after the 1066 conquest, Norman architecture was improving. The walls were less massive, and the Gothic or pointed arch brought elegance and height. The presbytery of Chichester Cathedral and the tower of Climping are examples of Transition-Norman style. Boxgroves's handsome choir shows the passing from Transition-Norman to Early English.

The vertical emphasis of the Gothic style was developed and perfected towards the end of the twelfth century. This is Early English or lancet architecture. It has a lightness and simplicity, with slender towers and larger lancet windows. Climping, Apuldram and Chidham are in this style. Burpham and Wisborough Green have Early English chancels. Boxgrove choir has deep mouldings typical of this period.

Further development of the lancet came in the Decorated period, in the 13th and 14th centuries. Stone vaulting became more complex and window tracery more ornate. From 1260 to 1315 the tracery was geometrical, as in the west windows of South Harting Church. From 1315 to 1360 the tracery was more curved, as in the south and west nave windows of Heyshott.

The Perpendicular period (1360 to 1485) is known for its straight lines, both upright and horizontal. Several church towers and some doors and windows are in this style and we are fortunate to have one church, Arundel St Nicholas, which is Perpendicular throughout.

As architecture advanced, churches became larger with more generous windows and doors which made them brighter and lighter.

Features of Medieval Church Architecture

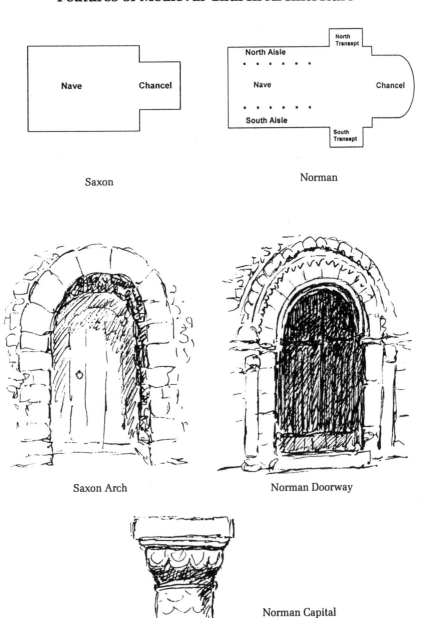

Saxon

Norman

Saxon Arch

Norman Doorway

Norman Capital

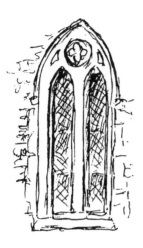

Early English Window

Decorated Window

Later Decorated Window

Perpendicular Window

Perpendicular Doorway

Perpendicular Tower

10 Walks near Chichester

The sea has claimed an ancient Cathedral City

Walk 1: Pagham Harbour, Church Norton and Sidlesham

Beginning at Pagham Harbour Visitor Centre, you have the choice of a shorter route which takes you to the church at Church Norton and back, or continuing from Church Norton to visit Sidlesham Church and the church at Pagham, before returning to the Visitor Centre.

Starting Point: Visitor Centre to Pagham Harbour, off the B2145 between Sidlesham and Selsey. GR 856964. Map: OS Explorer 120.

Distance: 3 miles to Church Norton and back, 7 miles to Sidlesham and Pagham.

Terrain: Flat, harbour walks.

Local Information: The Visitor Centre, just south of Sidlesham, has a car park and provides information on the history and wild life of Pagham Harbour.

The Churches

Church Norton: This may be the site of the first cathedral built in Sussex. Wilfrid brought Christianity to Sussex, sailing to Selsey in AD681. The sea has changed the shape of the coast – some say it has claimed an ancient cathedral city. It is said that bells can be heard ringing under the water on wild nights. The 13th-century chancel is all that remains after the Victorians took the nave and early Norman font to St Peter's Church, Selsey.

Sidlesham, St Mary: A light, spacious church, built in 1220 in Early English style, it reflects the affluence of the town. Sidlesham benefited from having a port, until storms in 1341 closed the harbour apart from a narrow gap, 'the lagoon'.

Pagham, St Thomas à Becket: First built in Saxon times, the church was the centre of a busy farming and marketing community. The port of Pagham was the ninth largest in England, but the 1341 gales ended this. Pagham Church was enlarged and dedicated to Archbishop Thomas after he was murdered in 1170. It now has pointed arches in Early English style and has kept its Norman font. In 1836 the Victorians restored the then dilapidated church. Saxon stones are under the table in the south transept.

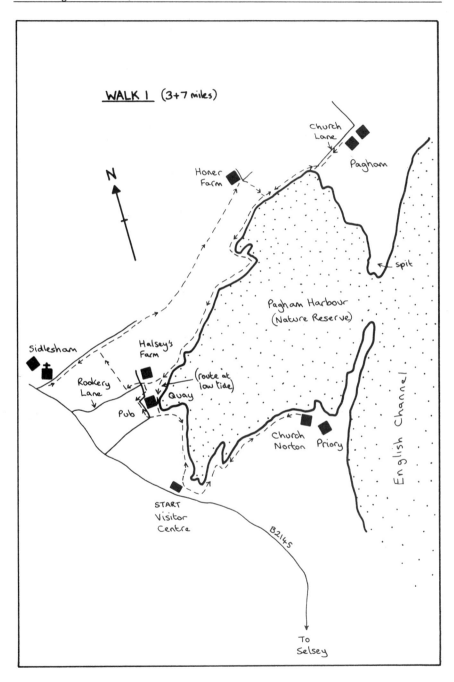

The Walk

From the Visitor Centre, head south parallel to the B2145 for 100 metres. After the water gate, turn left on to a bank which follows the edge of the harbour. The banks are lined with birdwatchers who will direct you if in doubt. Pagham Church can be spied across the water, to the north-east.

In half a mile the path curves south-east and onto the pebble beach. Church Norton is behind the hedge on your right. The open sea is 100 metres ahead over a pebble bank. First turn right up a track leading to the church car park. It was in this area that Christianity first came to Sussex.

To complete the 3-mile walk, retrace your steps to the Visitor Centre.

For the longer walk, return to the Visitor Centre and go behind it to head north-east along the smooth track. After a gate turn left to Sidlesham Quay. Turn right and walk past the pub, through the village and follow the road as it turns sharp left. After Rookery Farm turn right on a path towards a barn and over fields to a farm track. Turn left on to the track and Sidlesham Church is ahead on the right.

From the church, return east along the farm track, passing the path which brought you here, now on your right. At the end of the farm track continue east over fields and streams. The spire of Pagham Church is ahead. In over half a mile you reach Honer Farm. At cross paths here, turn right and south down to the nearby Pagham Harbour.

At the harbour, turn left on to the bank and walk towards Pagham. The church is at the end of Church Lane. After your visit, to return to the Visitor Centre, retrace your steps back along the harbour wall. Instead of turning up to Honer Farm, keep straight on and follow the harbour path as it curves west-south-west to Sidlesham Quay and the original track. At high tide you have to turn right to Halsey's Farm. An information panel is at this turning. From the Quay retrace your steps to the Visitor Centre. Do not forget to turn right at the gate!

Walk 2: Birdham, Itchenor and West Wittering

For a long section of this route you will be walking with fields on one side and water on the other — very peaceful and relaxing.

Starting Point: Birdham Church, off the A286 Chichester to Wittering Road. GR 823003. Map: OS Explorer 120.

Distance: 8-9 miles

Terrain: Flat, harbour walk.

The Churches

Birdham, St James: Caedwaller, the king of Wessex, after gaining power with bloody battles, turned to piety and made generous bequests to the churches. In AD683 he granted Birdham to St Wilfrid. The present church, Early English and restored in 1883, would not be recognised by either man. It stands at crossroads among affluent houses. The chancel arch is early 14th century and the sturdy tower was added in 1545.

Itchenor, St Nicholas: The Saxon name Itchenor means 'Icca's shore'. This little, Early English church is half a mile from the shore outside this popular sailing village. In 1175 the Bishop of Chichester allowed Hugh Esturmy, Lord of the Manor, to build a chapel here. The present building with porch and lychgate is a welcome haven.

West Wittering, St Peter and St Paul: In 774 Ethelbert, the king of the South Saxons granted land in 'Wystrings' for a church. The Saxon cross still stands. St Richard of Chichester is said to have built the present church in the 13th century. The nave and arcade are Transition Norman. There are unusual foliage carvings on the pillars of the nave arcade. The chancel arch is Early English. The 13th-century bell tower stands off from the main building.

The Walk

From Birdham church, head west through suburban villas. The 'No Through Road' becomes a concrete track to Westlands Farm. A channel of Chichester Harbour is on your right and sails of boats can be seen

Itchenor: St Nicholas

floating past. Keep to the footpath just south of the farm. At cross-paths take the left hand one, following the hedge. This continues west across a field for half a mile. When you meet the road down to Itchenor Quay, turn right and the church is 100 metres along on the right. It has a commanding position above a bend in the road, separate and tranquil.

After visiting the church, retrace your steps for 50 metres and cross to a footpath opposite. This heads south under hedges bounding houses on the left then crosses an open field to a farm road – turn sharp left here. Make your way through Redlands Farm, mainly exclusive residential. Once you have battled through this part, you reach a green lane marked to West Wittering.

Follow this lane as it curves north then south along a well-defined, wide track. Ignore paths to the right and left. In a mile you reach the main B2179 to West Wittering. Go south along this road, passing a caravan park, shops and houses. In about half a mile turn right at toilets. Follow the sign to the church.

Behind the church is a footpath across a field to Coastguard Lane. Turn right here and pass the sailing club on your way to the harbour. If you wish to see the coast turn left here. Otherwise, turn right and follow the Harbour Path, heading north and west for two and a half miles, in

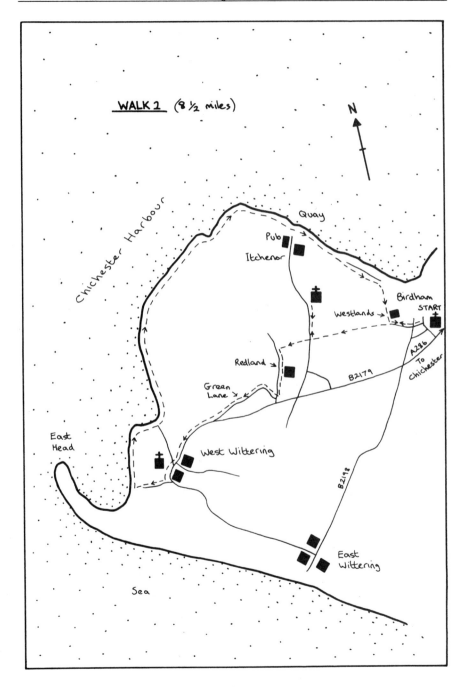

WALK 2 (8 ½ miles)

N

Chichester Harbour

Quay

Pub

Itchenor

Birdham
START

Westlands

A286
To
Chichester

Redland

B2179

Green
Lane

East
Head

West Wittering

B2198

East
Wittering

Sea

and out of low trees and bushes. There are glimpses of water to your left and fields to your right. Habitations are rare. Eventually you reach Itchenor Quay, with the pub 50 metres up the main road.

From the quay, resume the Harbour Path. Pass the sailing club then turn inland towards large houses with their own jetties. At their service road, turn left between the houses. At the end of the road turn right, skirting a small wood, then strike out across fields back to Westlands Farm. Keep heading east for Birdham Church.

Wittering: St Peter and St Paul

Walk 3: Chichester, Bosham and Fishbourne

A rewarding walk to an ancient cathedral and a particularly fine harbour church.

Starting Point: Bosham Station GR 813054. Map: OS Explorer 120.

Distance: 5 – 6 miles

Terrain: Flat, harbour walk.

The Churches

Bosham, Holy Trinity: Dicul, a monk from Ireland, established a small monastery here in the 7th century, even before Wilfrid landed in Selsey. Dicul did not have Wilfrid's success in converting people. Eventually they succumbed and we now have a beautiful Saxon church. The Saxon chancel arch, horseshoe in shape, is similar to that of Stoughton. The nave is Saxon with aisles added later. The Saxon tower has one original window, small and high. There is a delightful 13th-century crypt. Bosham Church stands at the head of Bosham Channel, welcoming home sailors in the sheltered waters of Chichester Harbour.

Chichester Cathedral, St Richard: The cathedral dominates the coastal plain of West Sussex, and the spire can be seen from every direction. The first cathedral in Selsey was in danger of flooding. It suited the Normans to have a centre of authority in Chichester and building started in 1091, under Bishop Ralph Luffa. There was a fire in 1115 which damaged city and cathedral. This was repaired with generous aid from Henry 1. The pillars and arches of the nave and choir are of this Norman period. After another fire in 1187, a new clerestory, ribs and vaulting shaft in Transition Norman style have added a lighter, more graceful touch. The outer aisles in Early English style were added in the 13th century while the beautiful Lady Chapel is in the slightly later Decorated style. In 1861 the 15th-century spire fell down dramatically and was replaced in 1901. As a result of its eventful history, Chichester Cathedral offers rich examples of varied architecture.

The Walk

From Bosham Station, walk south past the post office and shops to the roundabout at the main A259. There is an Indian restaurant on the corner and you turn right here into Old Bridge Road. Cross the millstream

and pass some new houses on your right. You are on the old Chichester to Portsmouth highway. It narrows then becomes an access road to larger houses. It narrows again and opens on to another piece of the highway.

Here you turn left towards the harbour. Cross the A259 and descend steps to a footpath over a field. At the harbour turn left onto a raised bank. In winter you can spy Bosham Church if you look due south. Cross the millstream as it enters the harbour. Turn right after a stile, keeping the windswept hedge on your right, and make for the church – about half a mile away.

Bosham Church

At the first houses, you either go straight on at high tide or turn right and along the shore at low tide. Both paths lead you to Bosham Quay and church. Harold Godwinson sailed from here in 1064, a scene depicted in the Bayeux Tapestry.

After visiting the church, at low tide follow Shore Road past the sailing club. This road is flooded at high tide. King Canute is believed to have shown his inability to control the waves here. With his example, at high tide we shall take the village route along High Street to Bosham

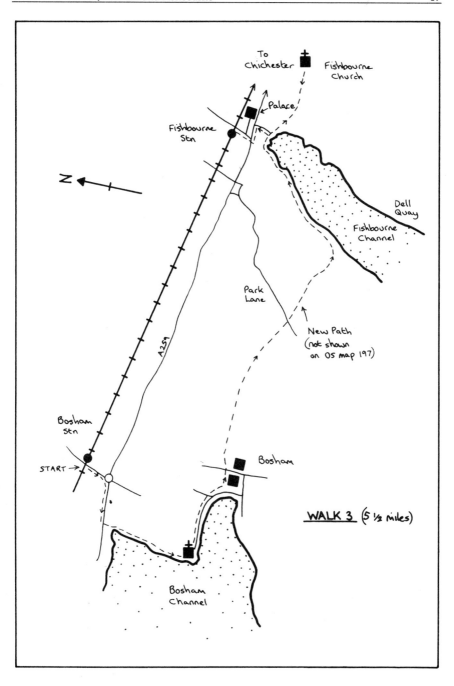

To Chichester

Fishbourne Church

Palace

Fishbourne Stn

N

Dell Quay

Fishbourne Channel

Park Lane

New Path (not shown on OS map 197)

A259

Bosham Stn

START

Bosham

WALK 3 (5 ½ miles)

Bosham Channel

Lane and the Trippet opposite. (The Trippet is a raised path by the harbour.) Both routes pass the pub. Keep going as far as the junction between Shore Road and The Drive. Turn left and find the passage which leads between gardens to Taylors Lane.

Cross Taylors Lane to a footpath opposite over open countryside, heading east for half a mile, with a slight deviation around an isolated cottage. Cross the next tarmac lane, Park Lane, and continue east with views to Dell Quay and Chichester Cathedral. At the T-junction of paths turn right then left to Fishbourne Channel. Go along the edge of Fishbourne Channel for half a mile then pass through reed beds to Mill Pond.

Turn left up Mill Lane, cross the A259 and turn left. When you reach Salthill Road, turn right up to the station. If you wish to visit Fishbourne Church, cross Mill Lane at the pond and continue east along the footpath – the details of the church are in the next walk.

Chichester Cathedral

Walk 4: Fishbourne and Apuldram

*If you can time your visit to coincide with one of the occasional opening
days at Rymans garden, this will be a particularly memorable walk.*

Starting Point: Fishbourne Church, south of the A259. GR 842044. Map:
OS Explorer 120.

Distance: 3 – 4 miles

Terrain: Flat, harbour walk.

The Churches

Fishbourne, St Peter and St Mary: Fishbourne Church stands between
the Roman Palace and the harbour. The chancel, built between 1243
and 1254 with lancet windows, was probably the original church.
There are crosses outside the north-east corner of the chancel. They
may have been made by pilgrims from Europe who crossed to Portsmouth and called at Fishbourne on their way to Chichester.

Apuldram Church

Apuldram, St Mary: A manor existed in Apuldram in the 12th century. There was probably a harbour village here then. Apuldram Manor Farm is nearby and Rymans, built in 1410 by William Ryman, still stands in lovely gardens. The fine Early English church overlooks fields to the harbour. There are signs of Norman work in the north wall of the nave and the square font is also Norman. The chancel, nave and south aisle are of the 13th century.

The Walk

Many paths enter the large car park of Fishbourne Church. Take the path nearest the church and head south-west towards the harbour avoiding paths to the right. After half a mile you pass a path to the left then take the next path left and south-east to Apuldram Church.

After visiting the church, go south along the main path, through the car park and turn left along a short lane which leads to Apuldram Lane, with Rymans, a 15th-century stone house, behind walls on the corner. Turn right away from Rymans along the edge of Apuldram Lane and right again along a track to Apuldram Roses.

At cross tracks turn left away from Apuldram Roses then, at a tarmac lane, turn right towards Dell Quay. The pub here is a popular haunt from nearby Chichester. It overlooks the harbour, Fishbourne Channel and is next to Dell Quay Sailing Club.

At Dell Quay, turn right and head back north along a path between boats and a wall. The path keeps close to the harbour's edge. You are walking beside the course taken by the Romans who sailed up to the Roman Palace at the head of the channel, over a mile from Dell Quay. Unfortunately, the palace is hidden behind 20th-century buildings.

Make towards flat-roofed buildings then turn right short of them and walk back through the meadow to Fishbourne Church.

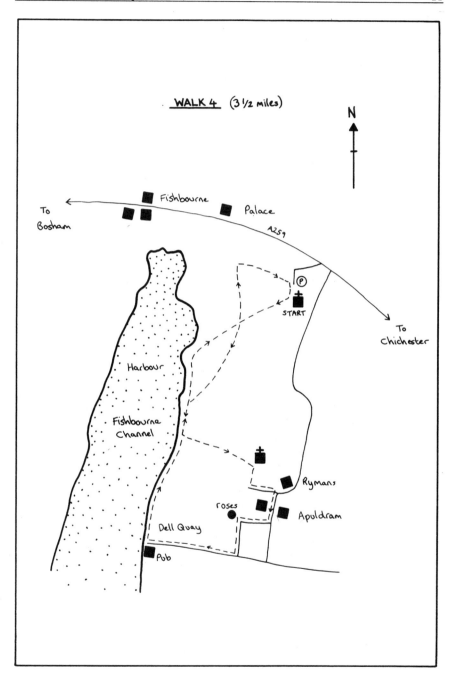

WALK 4 (3 ½ miles)

N

To Bosham

Fishbourne

Palace

A259

To Chichester

P

START

Harbour

Fishbourne Channel

Rymans

roses

Apuldram

Dell Quay

Pub

Walk 5: Prinsted, Chidham and Southbourne

Efforts to enclose Prinsted Channel in order to reclaim land failed in 1870. The sea prevailed, and today we can enjoy our harbour walk. There is an optional extension to this walk which allows you to visit the church on Thorney Island – a true island in the past, but no longer.

Starting Point: Prinsted Harbour, south of the A259, near Southbourne. GR 766051. Map: OS Explorer 120.

Distance: 5 miles, with an optional 3-mile extension to visit Thorney Church.

Terrain: Flat, harbour walk.

The Churches

Chidham, possibly dedicated to **St Mary:** In a peaceful corner of Chidham, this unspoilt Early English Church stands on the site of an earlier wooden one. The Saxon font has the marks of hasps under its cover. It would have been locked to prevent witches stealing the holy water. The north aisle is a 14th-century addition. It was dedicated to St Cuthman and pilgrims to the saint have marked crosses on the pillars. The legend of St Cuthman, AD681, is that he left home in Chidham and became a mendicant. Greatly to his credit, he took his paralysed mother along, pushing her in a wheelbarrow! Henry V111 stopped pilgrims from visiting St Cuthman's shrine. As a result the church lost revenue. It became neglected and thankfully, perhaps in consequence, no great changes have been made to the church.

Southbourne, St John the Evangelist: The architect, T. Chatfield-Clark, followed the Early English style for this church, built in 1876. The church is spacious to accommodate the growing population near the coastal railway. The new community centre caters for them today. **Thorney Island, St Nicholas:** 'Thornei' is mentioned in the Domesday survey as being under the jurisdiction of the Bishop of Exeter. Early priests would have come here by boat from Bosham. St Nicholas was the patron saint of sailors. The present Early English church is a long, single cell building with plain glass windows. The tower is late Norman. Harbour waters lap nearby.

The Walk

Facing the harbour, with Thorney Island on your right, turn left and walk along the harbour wall, heading east. Follow the coast for over a mile, passing three footpaths to the left. Take the fourth footpath, still heading east, away from the water. Primroses grow in the ditch here and there are the remains of poplars ahead. These are the sad remnants of fruitful vegetation in the not too distant past. There were hedgerows here, pastures, watercress beds, orchards and trees. It is shameful that

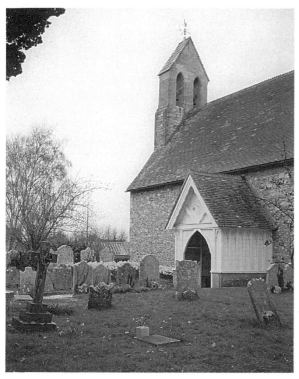

Chidham Church

the 20th century has left the coastal plain here almost desolate. The farmer has his monocrop.

The footpath leads to Cot Lane. Turn right here. Just past the lone house opposite is a two-pronged footpath. Follow the right prong, heading south then rejoining the road. The church is to the right round a bend in the road. Opposite the church is a footpath which leads further south to Chidmere Pond and the gardens of the beautiful 16th-century Chidmere House.

Back at the church, turn right and west, rounding the bend at some converted barns and the pub opposite. You are now heading north back to the footpath with the sad poplars. Turn left here back to the harbour. Turn right here then take the second path to the right. This crosses the field to Nut-bourne. Turn left at the village road. This appears to come to a dead end

Thorney Island, St Nicholas

at a walled house. Squeeze between the walls on a footpath which leads to one of the few remaining orchards.

At a T-junction of paths, turn right to the A259 at Southbourne. Turn left. Southbourne Church is opposite on a busy corner.

From the church, cross back over the A259 and continue west for 200 metres. Turn left and walk through Prinsted to the harbour.

For the Thorney Island walk, return to the harbour path and turn right towards Thornham Yacht Club. At high tide you have to divert through here and turn left on to a road which leads to a slightly sunken way back to the harbour path. Turn right and walk along the path as far as an army barrier. This may or may not be opened electronically by men in a distant gatehouse. Press the button, and with luck you may be able to pass through and continue along the harbour path to Thorney Church. To return to Prinsted, retrace your steps. In the past Thorney was a real island with a wadeway at low tide. The Romans never went to Thorney Island, no doubt discouraged by the mud.

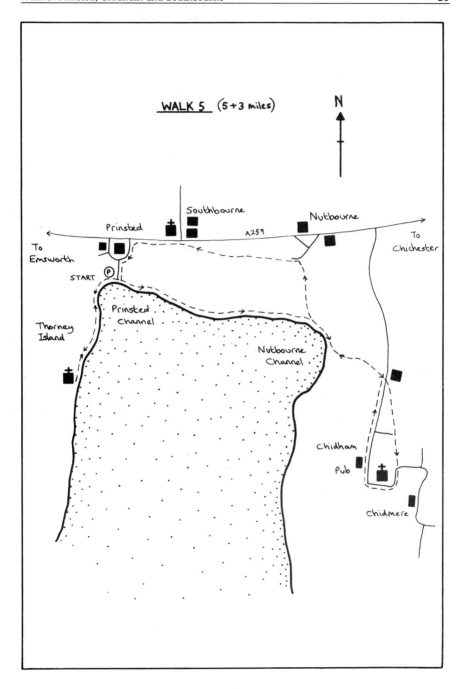

WALK 5 (5+3 miles)

N

Southbourne

Prinsted

Nutbourne

A259

To
Emsworth

To
Chichester

START

Thorney
Island

Prinsted
Channel

Nutbourne
Channel

Chidham
Pub

Chidmere

Walk 6: Sennicotts, Funtington and West Stoke

If you're planning to visit West Stoke Church on the next walk and don't want to visit it twice, there's an alternative ending to this route which avoids it.

Starting Point: Chapel Lane, Sennicotts. North of the B2178 between Chichester and East Ashling. GR 833070. Map: OS Explorer 120.

Distance: 6 – 7 miles

Terrain: Gently undulating, muddy in places.

The Churches

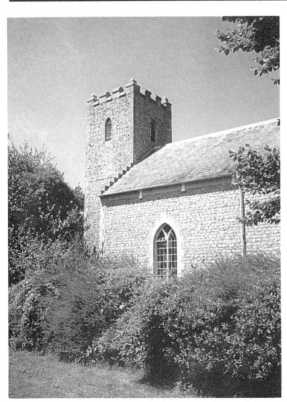

Sennicotts, St Mary

Sennicotts, St Mary: Hidden among trees in Chapel Lane, St Mary's was built in 1829 by Charles Baker, and probably designed by George Draper, a local architect, as a chapel to nearby Sennicotts House. It is a simple, well-proportioned building of local stone. Apply to the Vicar of Funtington Church for the keys. Inside, Sennicotts is light, spacious and colourful.

Funtington, St Mary the Virgin: Those who founded this church in the 12th century would not recognise the present large building. Only the north arches are original. The south-east chapel may be 14th and the tower 15th century. In 1850 the Victorians rebuilt the church in Early English style. The old yew tree (22-feet girth) may have been planted by the founders. Funtington is still a pleasant, agricultural village with village stores, farm shop, restaurant and pub.

Funtington, St Mary the Virgin

The Walk

From Sennicotts Church, walk north up Chapel Lane. Pass a solitary cottage at a kink in the track then look for a finger-post in the hedge on the left. Cross an open field making for the north-west corner, where the path swings back on itself whilst crossing into the next field. It soon reverts to its westerly course. Make for the hedge next to East Ashling Nursery and follow it to the tarmac lane. Cross to a path opposite which leads through several paddocks before sinking on to the B2178, nearly opposite the pub at East Ashling.

Turn left along the pavement for 50 metres then cross to Sandy Lane opposite. Pass four or five select houses and find a footpath at the end of the lane, beside a thatched cottage. This leads south-west over a firm track to West Ashling. Descend to a tarmac road and turn left into the village.

At the road junction, turn right past handsome, herringbone cottages and continue down to Mill Pool, where swans nest every year. Turn right here up Watery Lane. The footpath to the left leads north-west, directly to Funtington Church. However, you may prefer to continue up Watery Lane, passing Hallidays Restaurant at the top, before turning left at the main road. Pass the village shop then turn down the lane on the left to the church.

From the church, retrace your steps, passing the shop and Hallidays on your right. Continue along the main road to a lane on the left, forking away from the village. Cross and walk up this lane towards Woodend and West Stoke. The Downs are on your left. Just past the track to Downs Farm, turn right through a pig farm and the remains of Broadley Copse. Cross a tarmac lane and continue in the same direction, south-east, through Ashling Wood. After half a mile of straight track you come to a triangle of paths and decision time.

If you wish to leave out West Stoke, take the right-hand path, heading south-east. At the tarmac lane turn right to East Ashling then left at the main road. Pass the pub, and the path through paddocks is on your left. Retrace your steps to Sennicotts.

If you wish to visit West Stoke, at the triangle of paths keep straight on then turn left and north-east. At the tarmac lane turn left and follow it as it curves right up to the church. To return to Sennicotts, continue through West Stoke and take the second tarmac road off to the right. This is West Stoke Road (to Chichester). Go as far as a muddy track on the right. This is Chapel Lane. Turn right into Chapel Lane and head back south to Sennicotts.

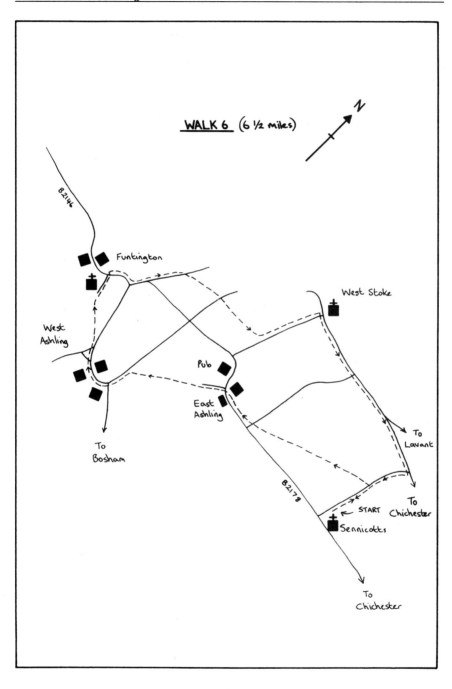

WALK 6 (6 ½ miles)

Walk 7: West Stoke, Kingley Vale and Stoughton

Farmland, woodland and coastal views can all be enjoyed on this very pleasant route. It also offers the opportunity to extend the outing by visiting Kingley Vale Nature Reserve.

Starting Point: West Stoke car park, near the church. GR 825088. Map: OS Explorer 120.

Distance: 7 miles

Terrain: Hilly

Local Information: Visitors to Kingley Vale Nature Reserve also use this car park.

The Churches

West Stoke, St Andrew: This church appears modest and unspoilt. There is a low tower and the overall impression is of a small building. It

West Stoke, St Andrew

is quite a surprise, therefore, to enter by the south porch into a spacious, lofty nave with mansard roof and beams. The nave is 11th century and the chancel 13th century. The wide arch in Early English style was built by the Victorians. It fits well with the lancet windows, one of which (in the west wall of the nave) is 13th century. The ground slopes steadily down from West Stoke, or 'Stoke Juxta Chichester' as it was known, to the harbour, about 4 miles to the south.

Stoughton, St Mary: On the other side of Kingley Vale, two and a half miles from West Stoke, is the downland village of Stoughton. Set back from the village in an elevated position is the white Saxon church. The herringbone flints are Saxon, but the cruciform shape suggests Norman influence. Inside, the nave is majestic, with Saxon height and Norman width. The handsome chancel arch is so like that of Bosham, it appears the same masons were at work. The transepts have Saxon windows in the west and later pointed windows in the end walls. The low tower over the south transept is from about 1400. The *Church Guide* gives a more detailed history.

Stoughton, St Mary

The Walk

There is only one path from West Stoke car park. It follows a track north between enclosed fields then through woodland and up to cross-paths at the edge of Kingley Vale Nature Reserve. Stay outside the gate and turn left on to a footpath, heading west for 50 metres. Then turn right and climb the sheltered slopes of Kingley Vale, heading north-west.

As you climb, keep to the edge of the reserve and turn left, away from the main path. This route overlooks a wide, farmland valley and the coastal plain to the south. Enter woodland and keep west, avoiding paths to right and left After 1 mile the path opens onto downland, with wide views to Langstone Harbour and The Isle Of Wight.

Continue west, down towards a tumble-down barn. At a T- junction of paths here, turn right and enter woodland. Straightway cross diagonally right, then turn left just in front of a gate. The footpath falls through the wood. Take care not to slip! This path leads to Stoughton Road. Turn right and the church can be seen up a lane on the left. The pub is 100 metres further along the road.

Retrace your steps along Stoughton Road, but only as far as Tythe Barn House, which you passed earlier. Here there is a flint track and footpath up to Bow Hill and Kingley Vale. A Memorial to a crashed RAF pilot of Polish origin is at the start of this climb. You soon climb up to woodland. Before entering it, turn to view Stoughton below.

At the top the track leaves the wood and you turn left along a wide, grassy bridleway between trees. Keep north-east for about half a mile. Bow Hill then shares its magnificence. There are ancient tumuli and spectacular views to Chichester and the coast to the south, whilst to the north Inholmes Wood and the Downs unfold. Turn toward the coast and head east over Bow Hill, above yew trees on your right and past a column of stones on your left.

Turn south so that you can see the bowl of Kingley Vale below, with a dew pond set in a natural glade cropped by rabbits and deer. Keep south down through the oldest yew forest in Europe. Make for the dew pond and carry on south through old, twisted yews to the reserve hut. This is the boundary of Kingley Vale. Earlier you were on the other side of the gate and stile. Cross back over to retrace your steps south to the car park.

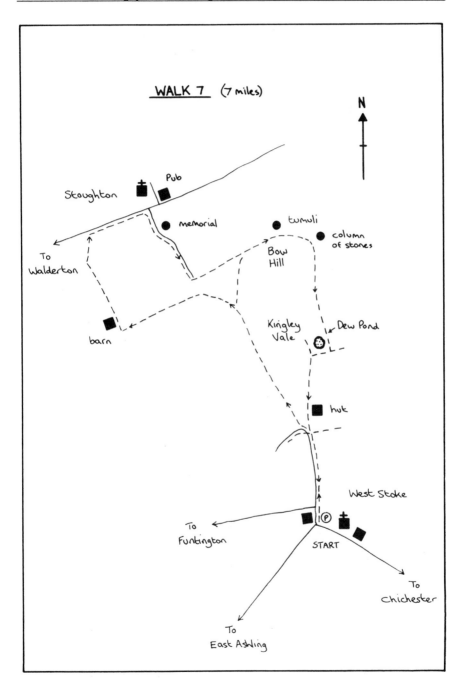

WALK 7 (7 miles)

N

Stoughton

Pub

memorial

tumuli

column of stones

Bow Hill

To Walderton

barn

Kingley Vale

Dew Pond

hut

West Stoke

To Funtington

START

To East Ashling

To Chichester

Walk 8: Racton and Stansted House and Chapel

Starting Point: Park Lane, which leads up to Racton Monument from the B2147, just north of Racton church. GR 782093. Map: OS Explorer 120.

Distance: 5 miles

Terrain: Gently undulating, some mud.

The Churches

Racton, St Peter: In the valley of the tiny River Ems, Racton Church is all that remains of the Saxon settlement. The church was mentioned in 1142, when it was given to Lewes Priory. Not much of the Saxon building remains. It is not known how old the ancient roof is. The nave may be Norman, the chancel and windows Early English, with the exception of the east window. This is Perpendicular, with 5 trefoil heads. It is claimed that Charles II stayed overnight in the handsome thatched cottage next to the church on his escape to France.

Racton, St Peter

The Chapel of Stansted: The present building is the work of Lewis Way who bought Stansted with money left him in 1794. He renewed the chapel and put in Regency Gothic windows. He then set out on the eccentric mission to convert Jews to Christianity. The north-west window, depicting the Fitzalan arms, was the inspiration for Keats' poem *The Eve of St Agnes*. The east window inspired *The Eve of St Mark*. The chapel is light and bright, the plaster vaulting slender and elegant.

The Chapel of Stansted

The Walk

Racton Monument is a ruined tower of ill-repute overlooking Chichester harbour. The lane up from Racton, heading west, is tree-lined and muddy in places. Keep going for about a mile. A view opens to the left. After cross-paths, take the next path turning right. Cross a field diagonally north-west, you can just detect the line across the field taken by other ramblers. At a post with 3 yellow arrows marking a T-junction, turn right. Soon you reach a car park and the driveway to Stansted House.

Turn right past the ticket booth and seek out the mainly brick chapel behind trees. In early spring, snowdrops and aconites, followed by daffodils, abound under the trees. The chapel is open some Sundays and during the open season of Stansted House. From the chapel, return to the driveway and find a public footpath which heads north in front of Stansted House and the cricket pitch. This path joins the main drive. Turn right on to the drive but do not go through the main gates. Instead, curve to the left and follow the road north. Turn right at some cottages. This firm track heads east, with open views to the harbour on the right and Lumley Seat on the left. Do not deviate from this track which, after cross-paths, becomes the tarmacked, tree-lined Woodlands Lane.

Eventually the lane curves right and offers fine views to Walderton Down. Go gently down Woodlands Lane towards the village of Walderton, and turn right at a footpath before you reach the main road (B2146). The path leads you south-west across fields above the little River Ems and towards Lordington Manor, with its grassy banks and masses of daffodils.

Cross the driveway and a bridge. The footpath is next to a cottage. Cross the field in a south-easterly direction to the B2146, where you turn right and south. The track to Racton Monument is ahead.

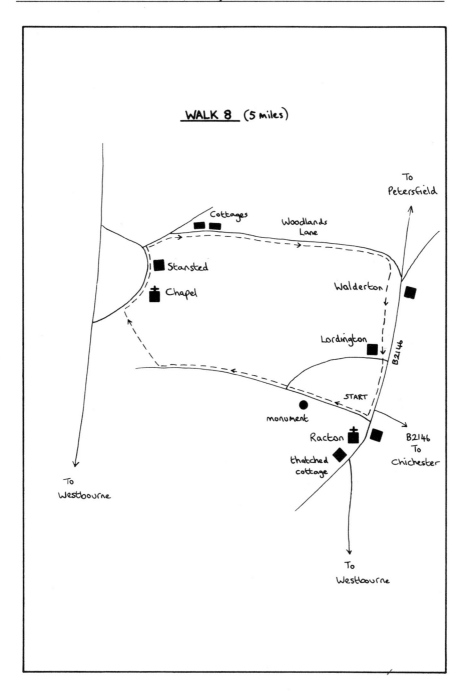

WALK 8 (5 miles)

Walk 9: Binderton, The Trundle and Lavant

*There was once a medieval village with its parish church on the site of the
present Binderton House. After the Reformation, the Manor of Binderton
passed from Tarrant Abbey in Dorset to the Smith family, who built the
house in 1677. Thomas Smith had the church removed as it spoilt his
view. A new, rectangular church of flint and stone was started across the
road, but villagers preferred to go to West Dean for services.
Consequently it was never finished, and when Thomas Smith died he was
buried in the incomplete church.*

Starting Point: Park in the lane to the north of Binderton House. GR 849109.
Map: OS Explorer 120.

Distance: 5½ miles

Terrain: Flat or gently undulating.

The Churches

Lavant, St Mary: According to Domesday, East Lavant Church was held
by the Archbishop of Canterbury. Little is left of this Norman building
apart from the west door, which has fine mouldings. The tower was
built in 1671 and the whole church underwent drastic Victorian restoration in 1863. This is still a pleasant, spacious church above the little
River Lavant, a winter bourn which only flows when there is enough
water underground to feed it.

Lavant, St Nicholas: This church is by a sharp bend in the busy Chichester to Midhurst road. It is usually kept locked and few services are
held here. It is an Early English church with a small Norman window in
the south wall. It was restored by the Victorians in 1872. They hid the
effigy of Dame Mary May in her negligée, originally intended for her
tomb in 1681, under the floorboards! She was not released until 1982.

The Walk

From Binderton House, cross the A286 diagonally right to a footpath
next to cottages. Before joining this, go 100 metres south along the main
road to see the disused chapel. Return to the footpath and head east,
crossing first the River Lavant, often waterless, then the railway line,
ever train-less. At cross-paths (4 blue arrows on a post)   continue

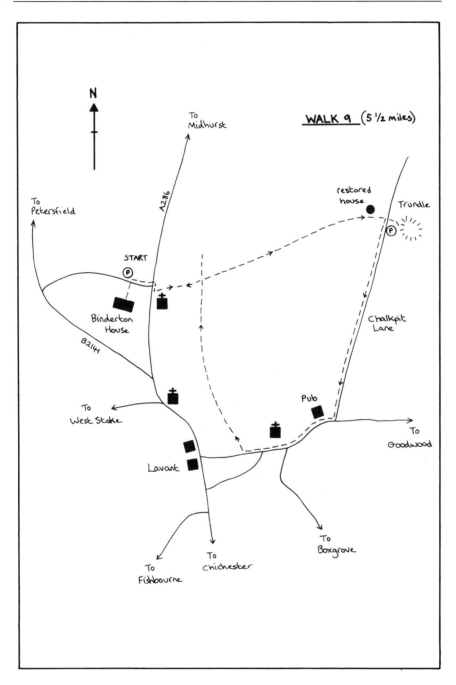

N

To
Midhurst

WALK 9 (5 ½ miles)

A286

restored
house

Trundle

To
Petersfield

START

P

Binderton
House

B2141

To
West Stoke

Chalkpit
Lane

Pub

To
Goodwood

Lavant

To
Fishbourne

To
Chichester

To
Boxgrove

on uphill, pausing to admire the view to Bow Hill behind. Pass through a field gate and keep going uphill with views to the right. Pass a fine, restored house on the left. The prehistoric hill fort, the Trundle, is ahead. Energetic walkers may wish to climb and explore this fine hill.

Otherwise, turn right and head south down Chalkpit Lane with wide views to Chichester and the coast. Beware the flinty surface! After 1 mile you reach Lavant and turn right. The pub is 50 metres along on the right and the church is a further 50 metres. There is another church in Lavant on the main road. It is usually locked and you have to seek the key holder.

After visiting the first church, St Mary's, continue west, cross the bridge over the River Lavant, fork right at the village green and turn right at cottages into Marsh Lane marked to Staple Ash Farm. This is the footpath back to Binderton. You have the Lavant and the disused railway line on your left. In a mile, at cross-paths, turn left back to Binderton House.

Lavant, St Mary

Walk 10: Stoughton Down, Up Marden, North Marden and East Marden

'Marden' or 'Maere-Dun' is Old English for boundary down. There were boundaries between the kingdoms of South and West Saxons. We cross these boundaries to find magnificent views and ancient churches.

Starting Point: Stoughton Down car park, east of Stoughton. GR 814126. Map: OS Explorer 120.

Distance: 7 miles

Terrain: Hilly

The Churches

Up Marden, St Michael: Closer to downland than to the village, elevated yet concealed, this church suggests secrets buried long in the past and undisturbed. In fact, one or two have been discovered: there are two chancel arches, for example, one supporting the other. The straight-lined Saxon arch may have been taken from the site of West Marden Chapel (demolished). Otherwise this is a Norman church with 13th-century lancet windows, all intact and all with clear glass. There are rumours of bygone villagers running riot in the churchyard. Let us hope that they welcomed pilgrims walking from Winchester to Chichester. Their crosses are on the lintels of the south doorway. All is peaceful now; the church and the English countryside forming an idyllic scene.

North Marden, St Mary: The church stands modestly alone between farmyard and fields. It is a tiny, perfect piece of early Norman work. It is a single-cell church with no chancel arch but with a rare beauty: an apsidal or curved chancel. Miniature windows in the chancel emphasise its shape. The doorway is of Caen stone with fine moulding and topped by a stone cross. Stone must have been brought by packhorse from Chichester Harbour.

East Marden, St Peter: Surveying its village from a grassy mound, St Peter's is at the centre of village life here. Crossroads below bring farm traffic, cyclists and ramblers. There is a covered, thatched well, a magnet for occasional visitors who chat or picnic here. The few flint cottages

Peer through the porch of Up Marden Church to a tempting rural walk.

seem as venerable as the church but the oldest is probably 400 years old. St Peter's has a Norman nave and Early English chancel. It is at least 900 years old.

The Walk

From Stoughton Down car park, turn right and walk along the road toward East Marden. After about 200 metres, take the second footpath left on to a track to Wildham Barn Cottage. Keep this on your left as you go into Inholmes Wood. Stay on this footpath for about 1 mile. Ignore all cross-paths, keeping to the left of the copse as you emerge from the woods, and proceeding to a pretty, flint cottage on your left.

Here you turn right and cross a field to and through Blinkard Copse. You come out on the north corner of the copse and continue over a small field, through stables and to the road at Up Marden. Turn right and walk up the road to a track and footpath on your left to the church.

Return to the road, turn left and, after about 200 metres, take a footpath on the left which zigzags then heads north by Apple Down. There are views ahead: right to North Marden and left to the recently restored

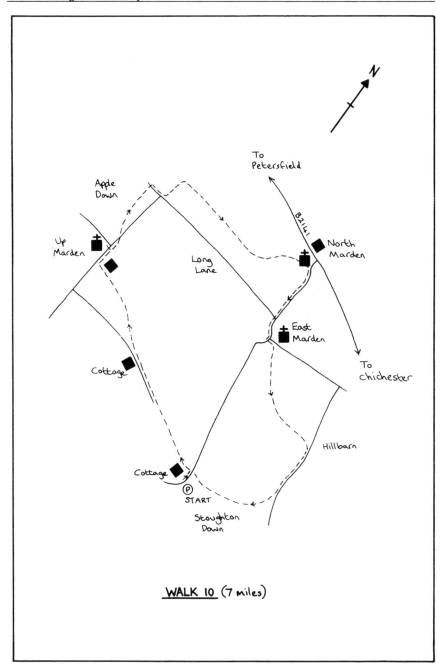

WALK 10 (7 miles)

National Trust house, Uppark. After half a mile you reach Long Lane, a tarmac road. Turn right along the road for a few metres then go left up a path at the edge of a field, with trees on your right. At a corner junction of paths, cross the stile and follow the path north-east, down through a strip of copse. Soon North Marden can be seen ahead to the left. First you have to descend to a valley, where you turn left. Follow the pre-scribed path at the edge of the field then go over a stile and up to the church.

From North Marden Church, continue on the footpath towards the main road (B2141) but do not venture onto it. Follow the lane round to the right past renovated barns and a Georgian house. The lane then curves down between hedgerows for about 1 mile to East Marden. Here the church is above a grassy bank on your left.

When you leave East Marden Church, turn left on to the road and fol-low it through the village. Turn right opposite a postbox and pass Post-man's Cottage, following a road which becomes a farm track. Keep south-east, passing the farm on your right. Ignore paths to right and left until you sink into Whitelands Copse. Cross the stile on the left and climb steep, open downland, heading east towards and past a small copse. Do not forget to turn for the view behind. A narrow path leads you to the track to Hillbarn. At this T-junction turn right and follow the track down through Wildham Wood. Look out for and turn right on a footpath away from the track. After a mile you reach the Stoughton road. Turn left here and Stoughton Down car park is on your left.

10 Walks near Midhurst

West Lavington, St Mary Magdalene

Walk 11: Singleton, West Dean and the Trundle

You can easily incorporate this walk into a fascinating full day's outing by visiting either Singleton Open Air Museum or West Dean Gardens.

Starting Point: The service road opposite Singleton Primary School, to the east of the village. GR 879152. Map: OS Explorer 120.

Distance: 6 miles

Terrain: Hilly

The Churches

Singleton, Virgin Mary: Both the village and the church of Singleton have kept their old charm. The outline of the church is the same as that in Saxon times but the aisles are later additions. The tower and the two-light window in the gable of the nave are Saxon. Stone to make the church came mainly from Quarr on the Isle of Wight. The village has its own fine flint cottages, and at the nearby Singleton Open Air Museum there is a collection of beautifully restored ancient houses and examples of rural crafts.

West Dean, St Andrew: This church stands partly in the grounds of West Dean House and partly in the village. The Saxon nave has blocked north and south doors. These would have been kept open during a baptism to allow the people to enter from the south and the Devil to leave the child and depart to the north. The chancel is slightly out of line. It has triple lancet Early English windows. After a fire in 1934, the church was made new and light.

The Walk

Facing the school, turn left towards the centre of the village. Visit the church via a short lane on the left then resume your walk in the direction of the main A286, Chichester to Midhurst road. Cross to the village stores opposite. From here the footpath skirts the cricket field and barn pavilion then crosses the wooden bridge over the River Lavant. This is a winter bourn and flows only when there is plenty of water underground. Climb the sheltered lane up to the railway bridge. Only the ghosts of trains pass below.

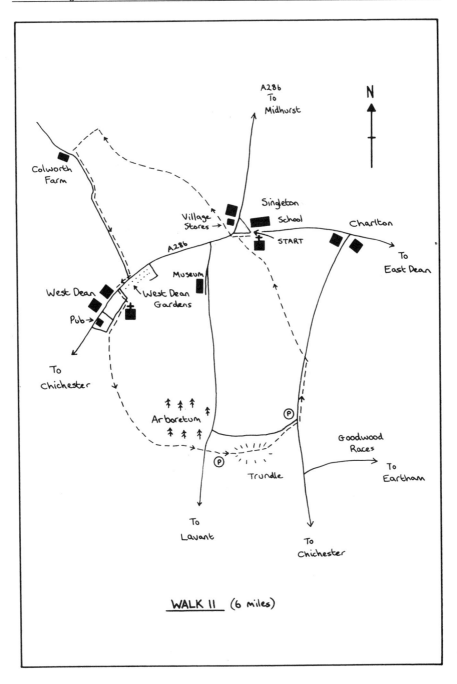

WALK 11 (6 miles)

After the bridge, resist the easy path to the right. Yours is the path which goes straight on, north-west, over the stile and up Hat Hill, keeping the pylons on your right. Turn to admire the view over to Singleton and Levin Down. Go under the power cables and continue north-west to the wood. Cross to the left of the wood and keep on course to the T-junction. Turn left to farm cottages and left again down the tarmac lane to West Dean, under 1 mile away – you will again be by the A286.

If you wish to visit West Dean Gardens (entrance charge), turn left and the entrance is diagonally opposite. You can leave by the church and continue the walk from there.

If you wish to avoid the gardens, turn right at the A286, walk 200 metres and cross down a lane leading to the church and village.

This part of West Dean is quiet and hidden from the main road. Walk south down the village lane with the flint wall of the gardens on your left. A little further on the River Lavant emerges and you walk beside it.

Singleton church

At the end, turn right for the village stores and teas; turn left, crossing the Lavant, for the footpath. This continues to follow the flint wall but uphill, in a south-easterly direction now. Climb for nearly 1 mile to the Trundle, St Roche's Hill, a prehistoric hill fort.

There is a car park on your right. Climb to the top of the Trundle, where there are magnificent views down to the coast on one side and the Downs to the other. Follow the track north-east with Goodwood Stadium ahead. Turn away from the stadium towards another car park, and the road down to Charlton. In under half a mile there is a stile in the hedge on the left. Follow the markers in the open field down to Singleton and the church.

Walk 12: Compton, Chalton and Idsworth

Allow yourself plenty of time for this walk: the spectacular views and fine, old churches are certain to demand your attention.

Starting Point: The village square, Compton, off the B2146 Chichester to Petersfield road. GR 777148. Map: OS Explorer 120.

Distance: 8 miles

Terrain: Hilly

The Churches

Compton, St Mary: Little remains of the original, probably Saxon church. A pointed chancel arch is Transition Norman. The south aisle is 13th century. In 1849 the church was enlarged, the chancel rebuilt and windows fitted in Decorated style.

Chalton, St Michael: High on the Downs, this church was an important place of worship and learning in Saxon times. It was the mother church to Idsworth and Clanfield. Early Christians called on St Michael to guard them. They feared Pagan spirits from tumuli, and devils not in Hell. The present building, early Norman with a tower in Saxon style, has walls which are three feet thick. Un-

Chalton church

der the blocked lancet on the south side is a leper's window, allowing the service to be watched without the church being entered and contaminated.

Idsworth, St Hubert: 'The Little Church in a Field' is all that remains of the hamlet of Idsworth, an ancient settlement on fertile soil. The chapel was originally built by Earl Godwin, King Harold's father. Edward the Confessor would have attended service here. The nave is in the Norman style, which Edward favoured. The Early English chancel, bell turret and porch came later. The chapel contains the only known mural depicting St Hubert. There are other murals of Salome dancing and being presented with the head of St John the Baptist. These murals were made about 1300.

Idsworth chapel

The Walk

There are two lanes which lead east from the village square to downland footpaths. The church can be reached by walking up either lane. Return to the square then walk north through the village towards Petersfield. Outside the village, there is soon a footpath off to the left. Climb into the field here and head west towards Compton Down. At the base of the Down, turn right and skirt it for 100 metres. Continue to a

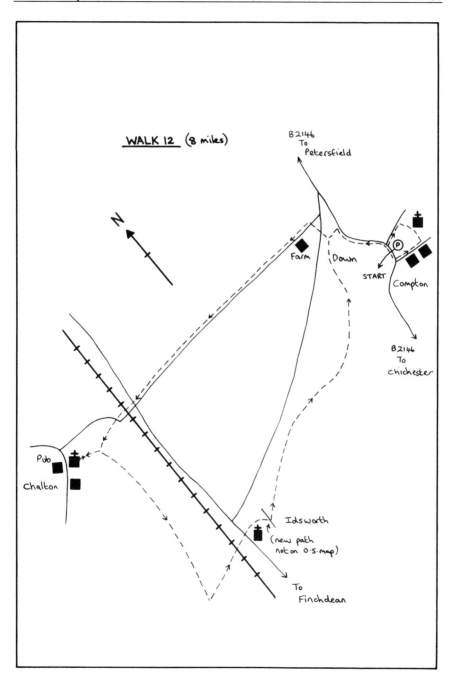

WALK 12 (8 miles)

N

B2146
To
Petersfield

Farm

Down

START

P

Compton

B2146
To
chichester

Pub

Chalton

Idsworth
(new path
not on O.S. map)

To
Finchdean

stile to a tarmac lane. Cross to the footpath opposite and continue north-west over the field, on a well worn footpath.

At the next road, Cowdown Lane, turn left and west. Pass Cowdown Farm on the left. The lane becomes a tree-lined earth track. After half a mile trees diminish, offering a good view south to the sea. Our lane becomes Huckswood Lane. After one and a half miles of lane, you reach a crossroads. Continue straight on and cross the bridge over the Portsmouth to London railway. The footpath to Chalton can be seen ahead at a bend in the road.

The path rises steeply up Chalton Down to a stile near the top. Once on top, there are fine views. In the distance ahead the windmill of Clanfield Down can be seen. Sadly, the top of Chalton Down is ploughed and no flora remains. To the right, Chalton Church can be reached by crossing a small, grassy field with tumuli. There is a picturesque, old pub opposite the church.

Return over the grassy field, but instead of taking the first path, follow the Staunton Way, the path to the right which climbs to the highest point. The path goes south under power cables, over a stile then past a line of trees on the right. There are fine views from this high path, not least down to Idsworth Church, standing alone to the left, below.

At a cross-paths, turn left and zigzag down to the railway. Pass farm cottages, cross the railway then the road and Idsworth Church is straight ahead. This church is a simple statement of beauty.

Behind the church is a north to south footpath. Turn right and walk behind the church. After 50 metres turn left towards the hanger which culminates in Compton Down. After half a mile the path veers right uphill, up some steps, then turns left along a grassy track. In about 100 metres another set of steps on the right leads you up into the woodland of the hanger. At the top, turn left into mainly yew trees. Keep to the top of the hanger, ignoring turnings to left and right.

In about 1 mile the path turns left downhill, continuing through woodland. It emerges, a steep, narrow path, on a grassy slope with views to Ditcham Park. Continue across the lower slopes of Compton Down heading east. The path draws you left to the road. Resist this and go down to your earlier path, which curves right to the base of Compton Down. Retrace your steps to Compton.

Walk 13: South Harting and Buriton

Both of the churches visited on this route are noteworthy. Harting's green spire is famous. Buriton's prosperity from the wool trade resulted in a particularly fine building.

Starting Point: The car park off the B2146, south of Harting Church. GR 784193. Map: OS Explorer 120.

Distance: 8½ miles

Terrain: Hilly

The Churches

Harting, St Mary and St Gabriel: The green spire of Harting Church is a landmark from miles around. Walkers on the nearby South Downs Way admire the view below and recognise South Harting from its church spire. The spire was dressed in copper in 1825. The narrow, Norman church was enlarged and made cruciform in the reign of Henry 111. It is a fine Early English church. The chancel has a high arch with dog-tooth moulding and a good triplet of lancets at the east end. Vicars of Harting have been motley in the past; two have been imprisoned for forgery, others upset the local gentry but one, Reginald Pole, here in 1525, became Cardinal Pole.

Buriton, St Mary: The prosperity brought to Buriton by the wool trade in the 13th century is apparent in this fine church building. Once the centre of the Manor of Mapledurham, the church included Petersfield and Sheet in its parish. The old manor house is near the church, overlooking Buriton Pond. It is a large Norman church with a fine, wide chancel of Caen stone. Unusually, the chancel has a wooden arch. The nave is Transition Norman with rounded pillars in the four bays of local greensand 'Malm' rock. The south aisle was rebuilt in 1300 and the north aisle in 1764. The 80-ft tower was burnt in a thunder storm in 1712 and rebuilt in 1715, but only to 48ft 6ins.

The Walk

The car park is between a recreation area and the church. The busy B2146 is narrow here with no pavements. This does not seem a very good arrangement. Hugging the wall on your left, head north towards

Harting church

the church. Turn left, away from the B2146, at the stocks in front of the church. Here there is a cutting between houses. Turn right at the end of the lane and walk downhill to the main road again. Cross to the footpath opposite. This leads north, up through fields to a tarmac lane.

Turn left on to the lane, which curves up around Torberry Hill, an ancient hill fort. It passes the old Greyhound Inn (alas, no longer in business!) opposite the turning to West Harting. Avoid this and carry on around Torberry Hill, which is on the left. This is the road to Petersfield. Take the first turning right just past Dell Cottage. You are heading north on a tarmac lane marked to Rogate and actually going to Quebec.

After 100 metres, at a sign for Manor Farm, turn left along a track, passing Putmans. The track becomes a footpath which heads in an easterly direction over flat, open fields. A kink in the path in half a mile is clear. You eventually reach a copse with lake below. Here the path veers right and skirts the wood before entering it and descending to Hurst Mill, a haven of peaceful beauty. Cross the water to the mill and follow the path up the driveway and back to the dreaded B2146.

Turn left along the main road for 200 metres then cross to a footpath opposite. You are now facing the Downs with Buriton about one and a half miles south-west. First you reach Old Ditcham Farm, which faces a lane with a fingerpost on the left. We do not go as far as the lane; our

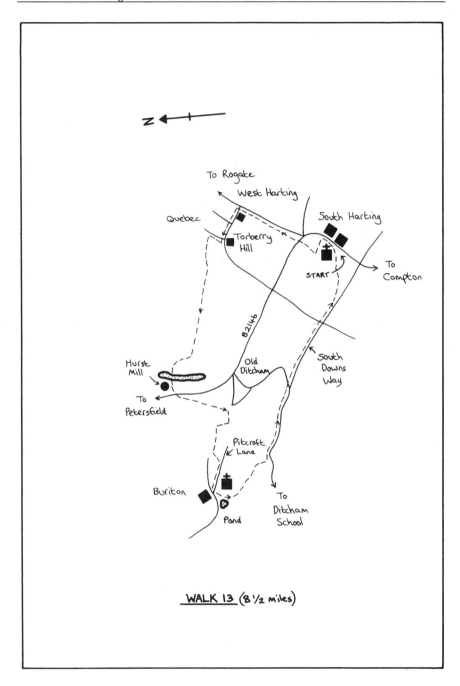

To Rogate

West Harting

Quebec

South Harting

Torberry Hill

START

To Compton

B2146

Hurst Mill

Old Ditcham

South Downs Way

To Petersfield

Pitcroft Lane

Buriton

Pond

To Ditcham School

WALK 13 (8½ miles)

path swings to the right through the farmyard. Head west, following the path as it turns right then left under pylons. At the barns of Cowhouse Farm turn left, skirting the farm buildings and passing an elegant, restored house on the right.

You emerge on Pitcroft Lane and turn right, passing one footpath, a wagon track which you ignore, on the left. At the tarmac road turn left. Almost immediately you come to a footpath on the left at the corner of the entrance to Buriton House. Follow this path as it skirts the grounds of the house and leads to Buriton, a popular and pretty village.

From Buriton Church, face the pond and turn left. Take a footpath south-east over fields towards the Downs. After four stiles you reach a T-junction and turn right up a track towards the South Downs Way. Continue south-east on a tarmac road which climbs up to a road junction. Ditcham School is indicated to the right. We turn left, down through what is almost an avenue of scattered beech trees, to Sunwood Farm below.

Opposite the farm the road bends left and goes down through woodland. We follow the South Downs Way, which branches off to the right beside a farm cottage. Keep east on the South Downs Way and avoid tempting paths to the right and left. Cross a track with houses and continue east until eventually you can spy the spire of South Harting Church way below on your left.

Turn left at a fingerpost and work your way down north and east, following the footpath which finally sinks into woodland and should emerge on the village recreation area with its lakes, swings and car park.

Walk 14: Cocking and Heyshott

A pleasant walk to two particularly interesting churches, and with the bonus of a truly magnificent view.

Starting Point: Cocking Village Shop and Post Office, east of the A286. GR 877175. Map: OS Explorer 120-121.

Distance: 5 miles

Terrain: One steep hill to climb and descend.

The Churches

Cocking, St Mary: 'Cochinges Church' is mentioned in the Domesday Book of 1086. It is another example of a church which has benefited from repair and restoration throughout centuries. For more details read Peter Leicester's fascinating guide, on sale in the church. It confirms a rumour I had heard that there is an underground passage (now blocked) to Cocking Church. It also reveals that the vicar in 1442 was a highwayman. Most of the church – the nave, the plain chancel arch and the font

Cocking church

– is Norman. The south aisle, east window, two decorated windows of the chancel and the tower are all 14th century. The north aisle and south porch are modern. In 1895 a Norman window in the south aisle was discovered. It shows an angel bringing good news to shepherds. Their dog does not seem particularly impressed and is barking at the angel.

Heyshott church

Heyshott, St James: In a rural community, villagers have to make a valiant effort to raise the funds to maintain their church. Here, in 1996, the money was raised to finance roof repairs. 'Hescheta Chapel' existed in 1130, when it was granted to Lewes Priory. The present building is 13th century; some of the original stones are in the south wall. In the 14th century the nave was enlarged. A potter's kiln has been found in the west end of the church. The wooden floor has had to be raised out of the damp gault clay. In 1885 the church was in a sad state, but with their usual vigour the Victorians rescued it.

The Walk

Walk east down the lane from the post office, passing through pretty gardens with streams and ponds. At the bottom of the lane, the path goes left and flanks one of these gardens. Climb the path and go up some steps to an open field. Cross over to Sage Barn, which you pass on your right. Further to the right are the Downs.

Continue north-east over fields to and through Hampshire Copse. When you emerge from the copse, follow the path down to the stream. Cross and keep on course to the edge of Heyshott village, with its flint houses, unbounded green spaces, a pub and, of course, the church.

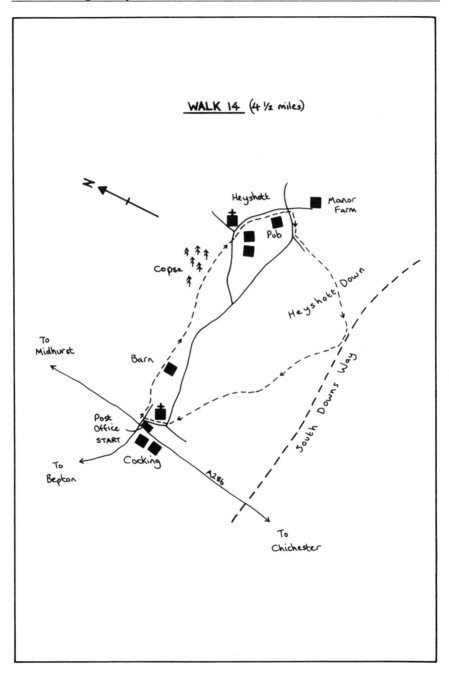

WALK 14 (4 ½ miles)

Your path brings you into a village lane. Turn left and the church is about 100 metres ahead. From the church, face the lane by which you came and turn left. Go past the Unicorn and through the village until you come to a sign to Manor Farm. Turn right here up a track leading away from farm and village. After 100 metres, turn right then left up into the Downs and Heyshott Nature Reserve, where there is a profusion of downland flowers. Stop to admire the view to Bexley Hill in the distance. Continue up through woodland then out into the light and brightness at the top of the Downs. The South Downs Way is 100 metres ahead.

Turn right on to the South Downs Way. In 50 metres turn right but NOT sharp right. You are heading uphill diagonally across an expanse of fields in a north-westerly direction, then down towards Cocking. On a fine day you cannot beat the views from this path: the Isle of Wight is far to the left and Black Down almost as far to the right. Once you cross into woodland, watch your step!. This is a steep and sometimes slippery slope down.

After the woodland there are more fields. You follow the hedge on your left downhill until you reach a gap in the hedge. Cross over a small field to a lane and stream. Cocking Church is ahead. There is a path through the churchyard to the first lane and post office.

Walk 15: West Lavington and Bepton

This walk is longer than most, but there is an opportunity to purchase refreshments en route and several excellent spots for a picnic.

Starting Point: Oaklands Road, (a turning off Dunford Road), near the church and school in West Lavington, south of Midhurst. GR 892206. Map: OS Explorer 120.

Distance: 9 miles

Terrain: Undulating

The Churches

West Lavington, St Mary Magdalene: 'I find nothing in nature so beautiful as the wooded parts of Sussex,' said Richard Cobden, the free trade advocate who chose to be buried here instead of Westminster Abbey. Gladstone came to his funeral here in 1865. The church had been redesigned in 1851 by the architect William Butterfield, later responsible for All Saints, London and Keble College Oxford. This church is of local stone. The timbers high in the nave resemble the hull of an upturned ship. The arcade is of smooth, hard chalk. The spire is wooden, repaired in 1985 after attack by woodpeckers. I heard the yaffle still laughing here. From Cobden's family grave on the terrace there are views south through the trees.

Bepton, St Mary: On the northern slopes of the Downs, Bepton drew its name from Babo. He came over the top around AD480 and drove out the Celts who had settled in this wild place amid stagnant marshes. Over 200 years later, Christians came from Wilfrid's settlement in Selsey to convert folk and build a wooden church. This was replaced, 400 years on, by a solid Norman church. The tower, with walls over 3 feet thick, was too heavy for the foundations and started to lean. It stabilised and a second storey, 8 feet high and 2 feet thick was added in 1250. The Norman tower still stands, with 17th-century brick buttresses. Also Norman are the round arches of the south and west doors. The lancet windows in the north and south walls and the tower arch are 13th century. The Celts and Babo would hardly recognise the drained fields and cosy homes among the trees of this hamlet today.

The Walk

West Lavington Church is well hidden but we have traced it to a cunningly concealed eminence on the south-eastern edge of Midhurst. After visiting the church, walk west along Oakland Road towards the A286. (There is a monument to Richard Cobden 100 metres up on the turning to Dunford.) Cross the A286 to a track opposite. This leads under a railway bridge serving the old Midhurst to Chichester line. At the end of the track you go through the garden of a pretty cottage then look for a fingerpost and stile hidden in the hedge up a tree-lined slope opposite. You are heading west and continue west across two fields to Pitsham Lane.

Turn right here. You will be coming back this way later so you may want to turn and check your route. Pitsham contains a rural factory where bricks are still made by hand. You pass it on your left as you approach a farm. Turn left through the farmyard mud, and go over a bridge and a stile and into open fields. Turn right and follow the hedge on the right as far as the farm gate. Climb up the next field to another gate. You are on a minor peak here. Cross the small field down to the lane and houses. In 100 metres you reach Bepton Road. Turn left and the pub is on the corner opposite. They serve tea and coffee among other drinks.

From the pub, turn right along Severals Road, passing a few detached houses then reaching woodland. Midhurst Common is on your right with paths to that town. We turn left at the first finger post. Once inside the wood, follow the narrow path. This becomes a track set with yellow bricks and passes through rhododendron groves. In half a mile, at a bend in the path, there is a choice of ways. Turn right and continue to the nearby edge of the wood. Cross a footbridge over a stream and you are in open fields with the Downs on your left. Cross two fields to the tiny hamlet of Minsted.

As you enter Minsted, you pass a cottage on your right and a farm track on your left. Keep straight on through trees to the tarmac road. Turn left here through farm buildings. Minsted Old House is on your left. Keep to the track which becomes a path and avoid all turnings to left and right. Pass through a gap in the old railway, the Midhurst to Petersfield line. The path becomes rougher with ruts. It takes a bend to the left then continues south-west for 1 mile to meet a farm track from the Downs. Pass New Barn, a pleasant cottage on your left, and start climbing. The track leads uphill to Linch Farm and a tarmac country road which links downland villages.

Turn left along the road. After half a mile it bends left. Bepton Church can be spied through trees below. Continue on the road which bends left. The lane to the church is on the left. You enter the church-

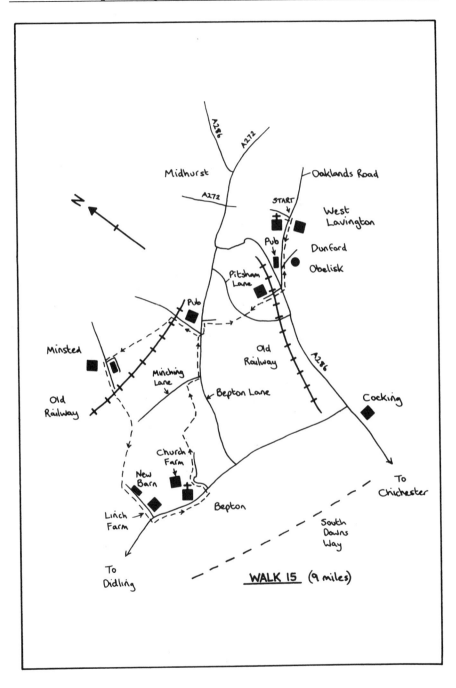

WALK 15 (9 miles)

yard by a gate next to a pond. You can pass through the churchyard (a good spot for a picnic) and out the other side. Go through the farmyard and down a track heading north. In half a mile you turn sharp right then in 100 metres cross a footbridge and stile on the left into a large, open field. Go down the right-hand edge of fields until you reach a cross-paths in the trees below.

Here, turn right along Minching Lane, which emerges at Bepton Road with a handsome Elizabethan house opposite. Turn left and go down Bepton Road, passing the familiar pub, now on your left. Turn right along the lane you walked this morning on your way to Pitsham then retrace your steps to West Lavington.

Bepton church

Walk 16: Harting Down, Didling and Elsted

Plenty of choice here – there is a longer, more demanding route or a shorter route in which you are walking mainly on the level. A further option on the more arduous route avoids climbing Beacon Hill, but it does add to the length of the walk. So read the directions before you set off then take your pick!

Starting Point: Harting Down car park GR 791181 **or** the lay-by at Knightsfield Cottages GR 803192. Map: OS Explorer 120.

Distance: 8 – 9 miles for the longer route **or** 5 – 6 miles.

Terrain: The longer route is hilly, the alternative flat.

Local Information: Harting Down car park is high on the Downs above South and East Harting.

The Churches

Didling, St Andrew: This church may have been rebuilt and re-roofed, patched and plastered, but it is a downland haven of great natural beauty. It is a simple country church, obviously intended for local masons, carpenters, shepherds and the like. All that remains of the Saxon church is a font made of Bracklesham stone. This single-cell church is now mainly Early English with widely splayed lancet windows giving plenty of light. The plain, rustic benches which are so in keeping with the church are also 13th century. The 17th-century balusters of the altar rails are so close together that even the smallest dog attending church with his shepherd master could not squeeze through. Service is by candle light.

Elsted, St Paul: This church is situated amid footpaths and faces south to the village, but is set apart from the main road and most of the houses. It has had an eventful and near disastrous history. The original Saxon building was what is now the nave and measured less than 10 metres by 5 metres. The Normans added a small chancel, a north aisle and the high, horseshoe chancel arch. In the 13th century the chancel was removed and replaced by another, larger one, with elegant lancet windows. The south porch was added in 1662. Elsted Church was neglected when a huge 'Cathedral of the Downs' was built at nearby

Treyford in 1850. Elsted's nave was damaged by a falling tree in 1893 and only the chancel could be used. Fortunately, 'The Cathedral' lasted for only 100 years and had to be destroyed in 1947 as it was falling apart. Elsted was repaired in 1951. Note the Saxon herringbone masonry on the nave.

'The Shepherd's church'

The Walk

For the longer route, locate the South Downs Way as it passes the north side of Harting Down car park. Head east along the Way, which dominates a rural scene to the north until it sinks gently into a wide valley, now National Trust land. At a cross-paths with a finger post set in stones carry on over Beacon Hill, keeping the trig point on your right, **or you may prefer to take the gentler route around the hill on the south side, adding half a mile to the walk.** After a steep descent on Beacon Hill, turn left down a woodland track heading north-east. Ignore paths to your right and left until you reach a clearing at the bottom. Follow the track to the left for 50 metres and turn right at the T-junction along a line of trees. This path leads to Treyford – there is a wooden statue of St Christopher at the side of the road on your right.

Head east along this tarmac road to Didling. At a sharp bend in the

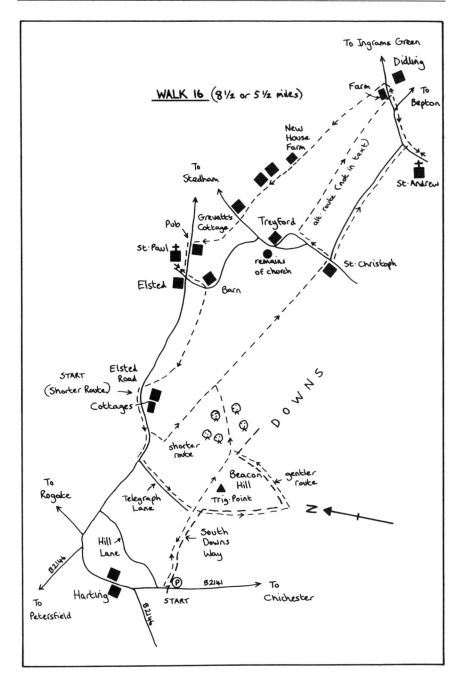

WALK 16 (8½ or 5½ miles)

To Ingrams Green
Didling
Farm
To Bepton
New House Farm
St. Andrew
To Stedham
Grevatt's Cottage
Treyford
Pub
St. Paul
remains of church
St. Christoph
Elsted
Barn
alt. route (not in text)
DOWNS
START (Shorter Route)
Elsted Road
Cottages
shorter route
Beacon Hill
gentler route
Trig. Point
N
To Rogate
Telegraph Lane
South Downs Way
Hill Lane
B2146
Harting
B2141
START
To Chichester
To Petersfield

road, turn right up a flint track to Didling Church, alone in the Downs. From the church, return down the track to Didling. Pass the Bepton and Cocking road on the right and Woolbeding Farms on the left then turn left. This path swerves then heads north, but we turn left and south-west after 100 metres..

Go over a hillock and down to a little wooden bridge. Then cross fields in a north-westerly direction for nearly half a mile, to New House Farm. Continue through the farmyard and straight on past a row of farm cottages on your right to a tarmac lane.

Grevatts Cottage is hidden in hedges on your right. Cross the lane diagonally to a footpath on the right. Ahead on your left is a low hill. Skirt this and, keeping in the same direction, cross two footbridges and climb up to Elsted, where the pub, The Three Horseshoes, awaits you.

From the pub, face the Elsted road and turn left. At the crossroads turn right to the church. When you have seen the church, return to the Elsted road and cross south towards the Downs on a road sign posted to Cocking and Treyford. Ignore fingerposts and turn right opposite Weir Field Barn. Once in the field, head west with the Downs on your left.

At the main road, turn left past Knightsfield Cottages. (This is where the shorter option begins.) Take the second footpath left. This is Telegraph Lane. It leads steeply up a sunken way between trees before emerging at the cross-paths at the base of Beacon Hill. Turn right and retrace your steps along this magnificent stretch of the South Downs Way back to Harting Down car park.

The Shorter Route

Begin at the lay-by at Knightsfield Cottages, on the Elsted road from Harting to Stedham. Turn left on to the Elsted road then left at the first footpath. This leads east, with the Downs on your right, towards Treyford. Continue the walk as described in the longer version, starting at Treyford and returning to the lay-by.

Walk 17: Midhurst, Lodsworth and Easebourne

The three churches visited on this walk have varied and interesting histories. Midhurst and Easebourne churches had other functions in the past, before becoming parish churches.

Starting Point: Midhurst, North Street car park. GR 887218. Map: OS Explorer 133.

Distance: 9 miles

Terrain: Some hills

The Churches

Midhurst, St Mary Magdalene and St Denys: Eight hundred years ago, a chapel of ease to the Benedictine priory of Easebourne was built at Midhurst, on the western edge of St Ann's Hill. The priory was dedicated to St Mary Magdalene and the chapel took the same saint. Since then the town of Midhurst has extended down the hill and the little chapel has become the parish church. The original tower still stands but the rest of the church was rebuilt in 1422 and restored in 1882. It is still pleasant to stroll in this old part of Midhurst.

Easebourne, St Mary: The church is situated about 1 mile to the north of Midhurst. Nuns at the priory are first mentioned in 1248, when

Midhurst church

Lodsworth, St Peter

the prioress was Alice. In 1535, at the Dissolution, the nuns were evicted and the church vandalised. It was not restored until the 19th century, re-roofed and the dividing walls in the church removed. In 1925 the tower was repaired.

Lodsworth, St Peter: The Manor House, with its own prison and gallows, is just south of the church. Down the lane and to the north is the site of St Peter's Well, visited by pilgrims for their eye troubles. It was probably there before the 14th-century church, with its tower of the same period. A stained glass window by A.E. Bass was added in 1968 and brightens the south porch. The window shows St Nicholas, his ship, three girls and three bags of gold.

The Walk

From the north of the North Street car park in Midhurst, step on to the causeway and proceed towards the ruins of Cowdray. At the River Rother, do not cross the bridge but turn right and head south by the river. Go through a kissing gate to a small, wooded hill, St Ann's Hill. One of the Bohun family, who lived in the fortified manor on this hill, founded the Priory of Easebourne. Take the right-hand path up the hill, continue up some steps, pass the fortress wall on your left and turn into St Ann's Lane on the right. This takes you into Midhurst and to the parish church.

Return to St Ann's Hill and take the right-hand path down. Ignore some new cottages on your right and keep straight on to a wharf. Opposite is a bridge to cross. Pass by a pretty cottage on your left and turn left round its garden. The path rises above the River Rother and Cowdray ruins on your left. The river winds away and you come to the farm road

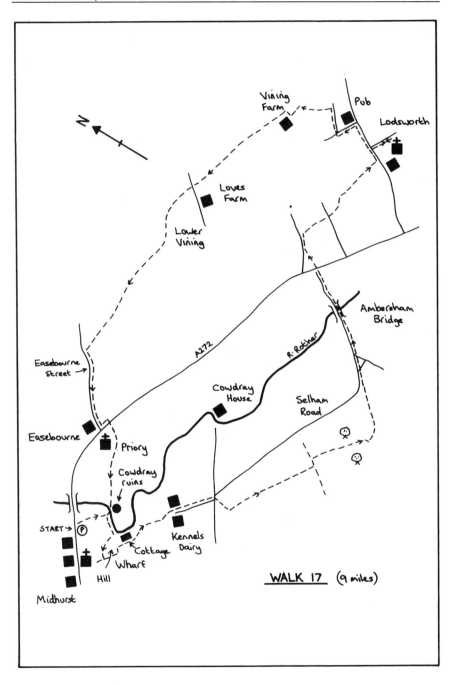

WALK 17 (9 miles)

through Kennels Dairy. This takes you down to the Selham road, with a private road to Cowdray House on the left.

Keep straight on. Diagonally opposite is a footpath up through trees to a sandy track. Follow this, as it winds left, right, left. You are generally on a south-easterly course. The path passes between woodland on the left and a field on the right. Ignore the path to the right and you come to Todham Rough. Here, at a T-junction, turn left. After 100 metres turn right through woodland clearing high above the Rother Valley on the left. The path finally turns sharp left to the north, going past swampy ground and a footpath on the right and emerging on the Selham road again.

Continue north on the road, bear left at grass triangle and go on to and over the ancient Ambersham Bridge. Once across, follow the road to the right past Moorland Barns. This road heads north uphill, cutting through steep, stone sides. It leads to the Midhurst to Petworth A272. Cross with care to the sunken track opposite. Still head north on the track for half a mile, until it joins a road. Take the footpath on the right here crossing fields with farms nearby and through a copse. Cross a tarmac lane and continue east. Opposite a hollow oak turn left and northeast to Lodsworth. Lodsworth House and village can be seen ahead. Cross a stile and keep the field boundary on your right as you walk down to the road.

At the road turn left to the village. The church is down a lane on the right with a half-timbered house and other cottages. Return to the village road. Head north and uphill for 100 metres to the pub. Here, fork left then turn right into School Lane. Attractive new houses share a green on the left. Just past the last of these, a rough track branches left off the road and leads uphill. Do not be tempted to deviate off the main track through Vining Copse for half a mile – until you reach a T-junction. Here, turn right then sharp left behind Vining Farm.

You are now heading back west, across high, open fields. Bexley Hill and its mast are on your right; the Downs beyond Rother Valley are on your left. Too soon the path turns left, **not** down the farm track to Loves Farm, but down the next footpath to Lower Vining. Its road stretches ahead down to Easebourne.

You emerge on The Street, Easebourne, and its chattering stream will accompany you down towards Midhurst. You pass many fine houses and reach the A272 at the bottom. Cross diagonally to St Mary's Church and turn right past Easebourne Priory. The path back to Cowdray Ruins runs south from the priory. At the ruins, you turn right, go over the bridge and back along the causeway to Midhurst's North Street car park.

Walk 18: Stedham, Iping and Woolbeding

There are two extra highlights on this walk – the 1000-year-old Stedham yew and the extremely picturesque Stedham Mill (don't forget your picnic).

Starting Point: The lay-by north of the A272, Midhurst to Petersfield road, on the edge of Stedham. GR 862219. Map: OS Explorer 133.

Distance: 8 miles

Terrain: Undulating

The Churches

Stedham, St James: The yew tree at Stedham has weathered its 1000 years unaided. The church, built of stones from a local quarry, began to sag and was rebuilt in 1850. The base of the tower and some ancient stone slabs near the porch are all that remains of the original church.

Iping, St Mary: In 1840, Iping Church was built on the site of the previous, presumably Norman, building. This, in turn, may have been on the site of a Roman cemetery: fragments of Roman vases and urns have been found. Iping is mentioned in Domesday and the Musard family held the manor until 1339. Today, this is a quiet, picturesque hamlet ruled by the Rother and its bridge.

Woolbeding, All Hallows: Certainly this church would originally have been built of wood. The flat pilasters or vertical strips on the outside recall the upright wooden beams. The church, mill, meadow and wood are mentioned in Domesday. The nave and the black marble font are Saxon. The chancel was replaced by a larger one in 1872. The tower was rebuilt in 1728. In its floor is a gravestone with a 13th-century cross. The porch was added in the 19th century. Stained glass from Mottisfont Priory has been put in the north window of the chancel.

The Walk

Walk into Stedham, passing the green then the church on the right, and continue down towards the River Rother. Just before the river, turn left along a riverside path which rises above the Rother. Soon the river leaves the path, which now crosses a field, with views right to meadows

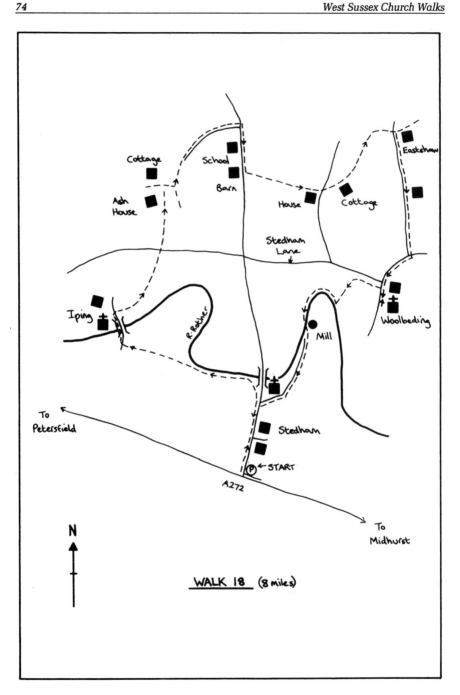

Cottage

School

Eastshaw

Barn

Ash
House

House

Cottage

Stedham
Lane

Woolbeding

Iping

R. Rother

Mill

To
Petersfield

Stedham

P ← START

A.272

To
Midhurst

N

WALK 18 (8 miles)

Woolbeding church

and trees. At some cottages, cross the driveway to the path opposite for a short, steep descent over cobbles into Iping Lane. Turn right, cross Iping Bridge and the church is on the left.

From Iping Church, cross the lane to the footpath opposite, heading north-east across a field with horse jumps. Keep to the right in the field, but do not be tempted down to the stream here. Cross a stile and continue to a narrow tarmac lane which you cross diagonally. The path now hugs an ancient, low wall on the left (not up the slope on the right). Soon you pass Ash House on the left and go on to a cross-paths in front of a remote cottage. Look for the narrow path and turn sharp right uphill to a T-junction with a track. Turn left along the track, for half a mile, passing a lake on the left. You then have views to Woolhouse Farm as you approach Tote Lane.

At this tarmac lane, turn right and climb the hill past a school and playing field. There are fine views ahead to the South Downs. Continue down Tote Lane and turn left at a barn and Tote Hill Cottage. Cross fields heading east to Woolbeding Lane, first passing a house and garden. Cross to Pound Common, with National Trust sign. Continue north-east on a clear track. Keep to the right along the edge of the common. There are views to the Downs on the right.

In less than half a mile a track crosses the paths. Turn right here, even though the fingerpost does not point this way. You can spy East-shaw Farm below and the path becomes a tarmac lane, Eastshaw Lane. Go down the lane in a southerly direction for about 1 mile. It emerges on Hollist Lane. Turn right down to Woolbeding. At the road junction, keep left past the farm and elegant Woolbeding House on the left. The church is close to the house, indeed, hidden by it. Turn left into the yew-lined walk to the church.

From the church, return to the road junction and find a footpath left, above Woolbeding Lane and heading north-west. This path borders the road until you have to descend to Brambling Farm at the road. Pass the farm then turn immediately left up through woodland. Cross the track at the top and then go down to the river. Follow the river, heading west, cross two wooden bridges and continue to the weir. Cross the Rother to Stedham Mill. This is one of the prettiest spots on the Rother. The road from Stedham Mill leads south past Stedham Hall to the church. From here, retrace your steps back south to the lay-by.

Walk 19: Dumpford, Chithurst and Trotton

There are two ways in which you can reach Chithurst Church on this walk, and it's certainly worth doing the walk twice and trying both – these two ancient churches are exceptionally fine.

Starting Point: Mill Lane, Dumford, a turning off the A272 towards Nyewood. GR 830219. Map: OS Explorer 133.

Distance: 3 – 4 miles

Terrain: Gently undulating

The Churches

Chithurst, St Mary: A place of perfect simplicity, Chithurst stands on a rounded hillock above the flowing Rother. Here is an ancient place of worship, possibly pre-Christian, certainly Saxon. The little chapel of Titcherste is mentioned in Domesday. The building itself is Saxon in shape and materials. The walls are of rubble and plaster with some her-

Chithurst church

ringbone in the north wall. There is a Saxon window in the north wall of the chancel. The plain chancel arch is early Norman. A 14th-century window is in the south wall of the nave. A squint in the north wall allowed lepers to watch the service from outside.

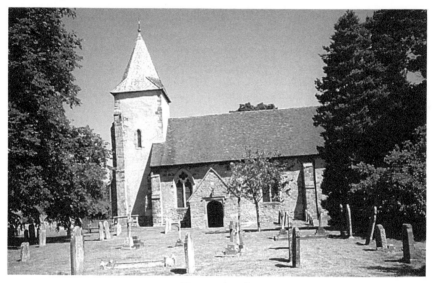

Trotton church

Trotton, St George: This is a large, airy church, really one big, beautiful room. There are four identical windows on the north and south sides in fine Decorated style. Grand, original beams span the roof. The whole building is unspoilt, remaining much as it was when it was built in about 1300. The tower is older, about 1230. The west wall is covered in medieval paintings. On the left is the evil man and seven deadly sins; on the right is the good man and seven acts of mercy. Figures in the paintings on the north wall celebrate the Camoys, who lived in the manor of Trotton. Thomas fought in Agincourt (1415). Trotton Bridge, which now has to carry much motor traffic, was built about 1400 by Lord Camoys.

The Walk

Walk up Mill Lane, past the intriguing Terwick Mill and over the River Rother with the wide weir below. The path leads north across a small field to Terwick Cottages. Here you join a lane which soon divides. Branch left on the main track to the A272. Opposite is a rough bank.

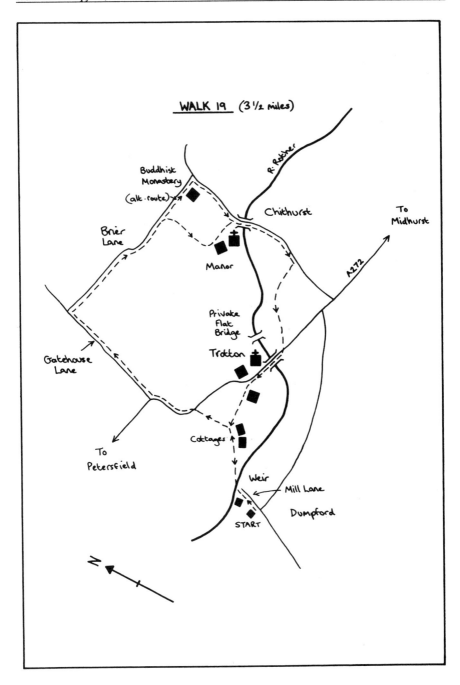

WALK 19 (3½ miles)

R. Rother

Buddhist Monastery
(alt. route)

Brier Lane

Chithurst

To Midhurst

Manor

A272

Private Flat Bridge

Gatehouse Lane

Trotton

To Petersfield

Cottages

Weir

Mill Lane

Dumpford

START

N

Climb this to reach a footpath along the edge of a field, with the main road on your left. Just past pylons, you reach a tarmac lane, Gatehouse Lane. The path continues along the edge of Gatehouse Lane but it is easier to walk up the lane itself. Ignore the path to the left.

In less than a mile, turn right into a hedge-lined track, Brier Lane, which has more brambles than briars. Ignore the path to the left. Where the track divides, you can **either** go straight on to Hammer Lane, with a Buddhist monastery on the corner, then turn right down to Chithurst **or** take the right-hand path winding through woods and fields with a final left turn down to Chithurst Manor. The little church is wedged between the manor and the river.

Turn right when you leave the church and proceed through the village for half a mile until you find a footpath on your right. This takes you diagonally across fields to Trotton Bridge. Not the flat modern bridge below. There is a stile in the hedge, which takes you over to the road. Cross the bridge and Trotton Church is immediately on your right.

After visiting the church, cross the A272 to the lane opposite. This leads back to Terwick Cottages, the weir and Mill Lane, Dumpford.

Walk 20: Habin Bridge, Terwick and Rogate

There's much pleasant walking through meadows on this route, and the opportunity for a reward of refreshments at the pub or shops in Rogate.

Starting Point: Habin Bridge, south of Rogate near Petersfield. GR 809229. Map: OS Explorer 133.

Distance: 5 miles

Terrain: Gently undulating

Local Information: There are verges, convenient for the starting point, near Haben Farm.

The Churches

Terwick, St Peter: Known as 'the Church in the Field', St Peter's is surrounded by sweet meadows and trees. In spite of the small, scattered community, the church is well cared for and maintained. There is a big, old cross now in front of the entrance and relics of graves, suggesting a burial ground here before the church. This was originally Norman, but only the west wall with its doorway arches and a small window remain. The main work, with lancet windows, is Early English. The old, oak door was replaced before 1907. The Wealdon Forest, stretching from Kent to Hampshire, was a source of building wood.

Rogate, St Bartholomew: The church occupies an elevated position at the crossroads at the centre of the village. It was Norman, but only one round arch at the east end of the north arcade of the nave is original. The church, which had become dilapidated, was restored, enlarged and had the present tower added in 1874. Fine timber from the 14th-century tower was used in the building of the new one. Remnants of the huge forest of the Weald remain in Rogate and Fyning Common.

The Walk

From the south side of Habin Bridge, an ancient, stone structure, take the track which heads east to meadows above the river. Cross the meadows diagonally towards the river and over a wooden bridge. On the other side go through a copse to a stile into more meadows. At the second stile head north towards the buildings of Fyning. Then turn right to the south-east corner of the meadow. Here you follow the tree-lined path which opens and leads to Terwick Church.

Take the footpath north through the churchyard to the main A272. Cross to the lay-by opposite and, still going north, take a track between a handsome house and a private road. For half a mile this is a sunken lane but then opens on to a tarmac road at Terwick Common. At a crossroads take the track opposite. This leads up under sweet chestnuts and oak trees, remnants of the Wealdon Forest. This is Fyning Hill, whose residents today have high railings, closed gates, alarms, warnings and guards.

Footloose and fancy free, we turn left at the tarmac road and follow it for half a mile before taking the second footpath on the left into trees. Descend on a sandy track through mixed woodland for half a mile, in a south-westerly direction. When you emerge you can see Rogate not far ahead. Take the track down to Rogate over an open field. Here the track veers south-west to the village. Turn left, passing the village hall, and go down to crossroads, with the imposing church on the other side of the A272. The pub and village stores are on the right.

Terwick church

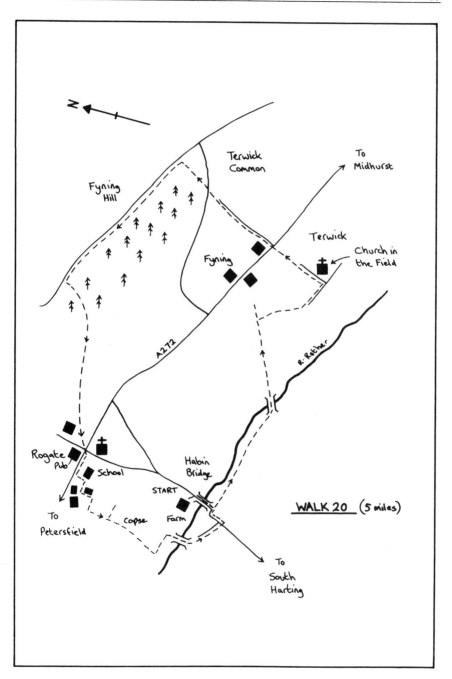

After visiting the church, return to the A272 and follow it west towards Petersfield for 50 metres. At the 'No Through Road' sign, turn left along a lane, going past the village school and through a small housing estate. Take the second road left through the estate into a field with a footpath heading south-west. Turn right at the stile opposite and head south around the edge of the field. Pass Souters Copse and go down to the River Rother. Here the path lurches left over boggy ground with a plank to the bridge over the river. Once across the river turn left along a dry, tarmac lane. Turn left again at the road down to Habin Bridge.

10 Walks
near
Petworth

Fittleworth church

Walk 21: Graffham and Selham

There's a more challenging option later in this walk. It's not the terrain which is more demanding, but the option may challenge your route finding skills – so bring a compass and give it a go!

Starting Point: The verge, Graffham Church. GR 929167. Map: OS Explorer 121-133.

Distance: 6 – 7 miles

Terrain: Gently undulating

Selham church

The Churches

Graffham, St Giles: Graffham village wends its way south up to the Downs. The church is at the southernmost end, where a small group of Saxon sheep farmers made use of the pastureland of the Downs. Nothing is left of this first church. The earliest part of the present building is the Norman west arches of the arcades. There is also an old doorway, possibly 14th century, to the vestry. It has a lock with the heads of a king and a lady in a head dress of horns. Between 1874 and 1889 the church, including spire, was rebuilt as a memorial to Bishop Wilberforce of nearby Lavington Park. He was the son of the great William Wilberforce who campaigned against slavery. In spite of the alterations, this church still has an air of antiquity and sits comfortably under the wooded Downs.

Selham, St James: This tiny church on the road to Ambersham is essentially Saxon. The plan, nave and chancel, is almost unchanged. In the 13th century a south chapel was included. This, together with the west wall, was rebuilt and a bellcote added in the 19th century. The rest of the church contains both Saxon and Norman work, suggesting that its origins are pre-Conquest, when European styles of masonry had already crossed into England. The round chancel arch is Norman, with amazing carvings of both periods. There is basket-work ornamentation on the north capital and on the south there is a snake chewing its own tail. This may have been inspired by the Viking serpents. Outside, the stonework is largely herringbone, either late Saxon or early Norman. Fortunately, the Victorians left this Church alone and it remains a monument to far earlier ages.

The Walk

From the church, walk down the village street with picturesque cottages on either side. You are heading north. Ignore paths and roads to left and right. The road curves right, past a war memorial, a pub and hall. At the shop, turn left towards Selham. Keep going downhill, past more scattered houses.

After Wiblings Farm and pond, you come to a T-junction and cross left to a footpath opposite. This is a sandy, enclosed path to Selham Common. Emerge through a gate and continue north over a field and down to a farm near Smoky House. The lane here crosses the old Midhurst to Petersfield railway line, and possibly the smoke from the steam trains has given this spot its name.

Turn right at the T-junction and you are nearly in Selham. The old priory is on your right, and further on is the tiny, ancient church. Just before the church is a footpath heading back south and passing the old railway station. Cross a field to enter a copse. Then there is a stout, wooden bridge and a causeway over marshland before you climb up to the tarmac road. Turn right and fork right towards Graffham. Selham House is on your right. The easy way back to Graffham is on the road.

The adventurous may care to try this option. One hundred metres south of Selham House, where a footpath crosses the road, turn left into Graffham Common. To avoid going astray, a compass would help. At a

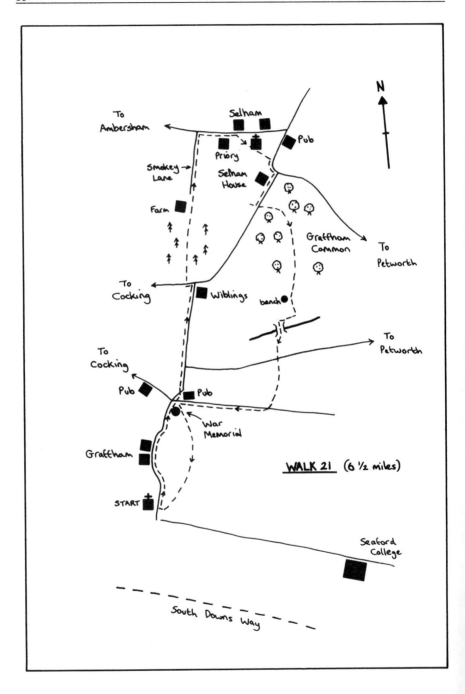

junction of paths just inside the common, turn right (not sharp right as this leads back to the road) and head south. After a left and right turn this path climbs up through trees to a sandy ridge with a fine prospect to the Downs. Keep heading south, avoid the many cross-paths. At a seat look for a finger post in trees on the left and find a narrow path down to a clear brook. Turn right and follow the brook to a little wooden bridge. Snowdrops hide here in February. Cross the bridge over the stream and climb to a field with a tarmac lane ahead.

The footpath opposite continues south. Keep straight on at a cross-paths, squeezing on to a path next to the farm gate. After 50 metres the main path curves left. You keep straight on through a copse and you come to a sloping field with a fine view over to Graffham Church. Cross the field diagonally down to the right and you come to the track which leads back to the war memorial. Turn right on to the track, go past a playing field and turn left, uphill, towards farm buildings. The path hugs the right-hand side of the farm and carries on up past the village school to the church.

Walk 22: Duncton, Burton Park and Seaford College

This walk visits two churches built in the same parish in 1866, and within a quarter of a mile of each other. Both are blessed in their different ways. However, the highlight must be the tiny but fascinating Burton Church, which is believed to have been built in the 11th century.

Starting Point: Duncton Primary School, Willetts Close, west of the A285 and south of Duncton Church. GR 959172. Map: OS Explorer 121.

Distance: 6 – 7 miles

Terrain: Quite hilly

The Churches

Duncton, Holy Trinity: Built by Lord Leconfield for the villagers, it is conventional Anglican in Decorated style, with a pointed chancel arch and a tower in the south-east with a small spire. It has a comfortable air of belonging to the people.

Duncton, St Anthony & St George

Duncton, St Anthony and St George: The Roman Catholic church in the village and also Decorated in style, it overlooks Burton Park, seat of the Biddulph family 1750 – 1900. In 1866 the Biddulphs employed G. Blount to build this church to replace the chapel in their Grecian-style house. This church has an air of beauty in waiting.

Burton Church: This church of unknown dedication stood in

Burton or 'Bodecton' centuries before all the grand buildings hereabouts. Its walls are of rubble, ironstone and tufa. There is herringbone work in the north walls, indicating its Saxon origins. This tiny church is believed to have been built in 1075, and there is a blocked doorway of about that date in the south wall. The square windows are of 1636 vintage and the church has escaped Victorian restoration. The font is one of the oldest in Sussex. The screen between the nave and chancel is 15th century. There is a 16th-century wall painting by the north window of the nave. A young woman with red hair is tied down to a St Andrew cross. She may be St Wilgeforte, who wanted to die a virgin. In answer to her prayers, she grew a beard and was put to death.

Burton church

East Lavington, St Peter: This restored Early English church is set on the wooded slopes of Woolavington Down. Now in the grounds of Seaford College, Lavington Park, this church still has fine views north over the Weald. Buried here are Samuel Wilberforce and his wife.

The Walk

Willetts Close ends in a field gate and a footpath up a gently sloping field and past the school. Set off up this path and turn right at the corner of the school recreation ground. The parish church can be seen ahead, up across the meadow. A gate in the boundary wall allows entrance. You may prefer to follow the main road to the church.

After visiting the church, leave by the other, main gate on a short road with a few houses, one the old school. Head for the A285 and cross with care to the pavement opposite. Turn left and north up to the Catholic church. Apart from cleaning on Saturdays and services on Sundays, this is usually locked, unfortunately.

Follow the footpath next to the Catholic church heading east and suddenly you are looking over Burton, with the Downs beyond. Just to the left of the converted Palladian house is the tiny Burton Church.

From Burton Church, face the road and turn left. Pass the house and turn your back on it. At the first footpath, turn left down through meadowland and leave Burton Park by wrought iron gates and a grassy bridge beside a large pond. This path leads into fields and continues up towards the Downs. In half a mile turn right through woodland and apple orchards. A short, steep slope leads down to a lane and picturesque Duncton Mill. Resist the temptation to go down to the mill.

Instead, turn left, walk up the lane for a few metres and turn right at a footpath to a field opposite. Continue in westerly direction until you reach the farm at the base of Duncton Hill. It is here that the original church of 1086 stood, with a Saxon village at Manor Farm. Turn towards the main A285, cross to a green triangle and go up the lane opposite. This leads past occasional cottages to Seaford College. Instead of entering the college campus, go a few metres up the wooded track and at an opening on the right there are some steps up to the church.

Return to the entrance to the college grounds and follow the driveway as it curves in front of and below the main house. There are views north over the sweep of the woods and meadows down to Petworth. Carry on west on the drive, past the assembly hall and other school buildings. As you leave the campus at a cross-tracks, turn right and go down a slope away from Seaford College, heading north. The track becomes a tarmac road through woodland. It curves left. You go past Lavington Stud on the left and 50 metres on turn right into woodland.

This path soon leaves the woodland. It passes Upperbarn House and a footpath on the left and leads up to a T-junction at the edge of another wood. Turn right here, skirt the wood and go through farm buildings along a track which leads to Westerlands Stud. This is a large, opulent, red-brick house. The path curves right past the barn, then left away from the house through a circumscribed route between horse paddocks and polo fields. You escape these as you continue east on a wide, open field with Ducton Roman Catholic Church way ahead.

Pass Ridlington Farm and in 100 metres turn right towards the Downs. At the next field cross diagonally uphill and south-east to a gate on the low ridge. Below is the primary school and Willetts Close.

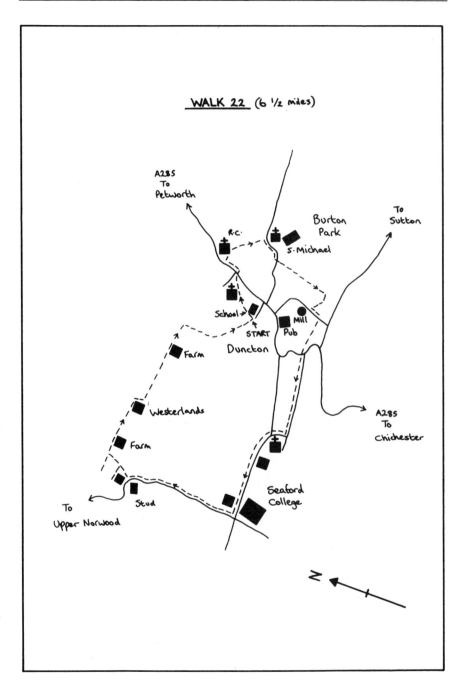

Walk 23: Burton Park, Barlavington, Sutton and Coates

This walk gives the option of visiting just the first three churches or making a two-mile extension to see Coates Church.

Starting Point: Burton Mill Pond, 1 mile east of the A285. GR 979181. Map: OS Explorer 121.

Distance: 6 miles or 8 miles

Terrain: Gently undulating

Local Information: Burton Mill Pond is quite large and picturesque. Opposite, the mill stands in a hollow, and there is room for a few cars to park.

Burlavington church

The Churches

Burton Park is described in the previous walk.

Barlavington, St Mary: The church faces the wooded slopes of the Downs and backs onto a farmyard. In medieval times the farm must have employed more people. The church is not small. It is a simple building of local Greensand stone. Originally Norman, the west window and south arcade are Transition-Norman. The other windows are Early English. Victorian restoration in 1879 kept to the Early English style. The greatest treasure of this church is its position in the rolling Sussex countryside, a walker's haven.

Sutton, St John the Baptist: Sutton tower can be seen from Barlavington. The two churches, physically so close, are poles apart. Sutton village is a varied, active community and the church is central to it. This large church has examples of architecture from throughout the ages. Herringbone masonry in the north wall suggests the first church was Saxon. The nave is Norman with solid, round pillars. The chancel is Decorated and has a chancel arch of the same period.

Coates, St Agatha: The church and manor house, a handsome 17th-century building, nestle together on a gentle heath slope. The Norman church was dark with small, round-headed windows. In the 13th century Lewes Priory took it over and added Early English lancets. One of the original windows is central in the south wall of the nave. The 16th-century door on the north side gives access to the manor.

Coates church

The Walk

From the hollow at Burton Mill, go up to the road and turn right. Cross to the footpath opposite. This leads through a nature reserve for half a mile. The path emerges at Burton Park, with the converted school buildings of St Michael's ahead. Turn right towards the main house, now apartments, and at the corner on the left is the tiny Burton Church. In February there are numerous snowdrops.

On leaving the church, follow the driveway as it curves in front of the main building. After 200 metres, turn left down a footpath which leads through a meadow and out of Burton Park through wrought iron gates. Cross by a pond and huge mare's tails. You then climb up towards the Downs for half a mile with woodland on your right. Ignore the path off to the right and veer left on the main track, up to a tarmac lane.

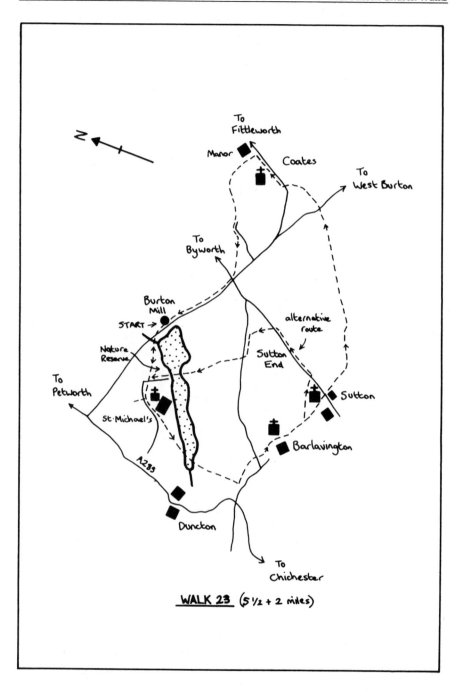

Z

To
Fittleworth

Manor

Coates

To
West Burton

To
Byworth

Burton
Mill

START →

Nature
Reserve

alternative
route

Sutton
End

To
Petworth

St. Michael's

Sutton

A285

Barlavington

Duncton

To
Chichester

WALK 23 (5½ + 2 miles)

At the lane, turn left on to another footpath which leads east over a field, down beside a garden. Here the path dips into another tarmac lane. Cross and climb steps in the bank opposite. Pass converted stables on your left and Barlavington Farm and the church are ahead, with magnificent views of the Downs on your right.

You can pass through the churchyard, skirt the farm on your left then turn right away from Barlavington. After 100 metres, look for a stile in the hedge on your right and climb over it to a delightful little valley. Cross diagonally towards a copse, which you enter via a footbridge over a stream. Climb up to the top of the slope and turn left at cross paths to Sutton village. The church is on the left, and the pub about 100 metres on the right.

For the shorter, 6-mile walk: Turn left at Sutton Church and go north along a tarmac lane out of the village. Ignore all footpaths until you have walked over half a mile and through Sutton End with its poorhouse. At a grass triangle on the left, look out for a footpath along a private road. The path continues through woodland to a tarmac lane. Turn left and walk along the lane which bends to the left. You keep straight on past a fine, old cottage. Keep on track through wetlands at the back of St. Michael's. Go past a few residential buildings, on tarmac now. At a bend in the lane enter the nature reserve and retrace your steps to Burton Mill.

For the longer, 8-mile walk: Diagonally opposite Sutton Church, cross the village road to a footpath which leads down a short lane. Cross meadows and go down over dry marshland. Follow fingerposts northeast and across a ditch to Winters Copse. Enter the copse and continue east through old and new plantations. At a cross-paths turn left on to the main, tree-lined track. Keep to this track, heading north-east and avoiding paths to left and right. Cross a tarmac lane to a track opposite on the right. This skirts the nature reserve, Sutton Common on the left. In half a mile, at the end of the wire fence, turn left up to a tarmac road. Here, turn right and walk along the road until you see Coates Church on the left.

From Coates Church, return to the road and turn left (in the same direction as before). In a few metres you reach mellow, stone Coates Manor. Turn left beside the garden and head west over fields and around a hillock to the south-west corner of the field. Turn right here and take the track at the edge of woodland in a westerly direction. The track curves left, but you keep straight on through woodland. As you emerge, take the left-hand path up over fields to a tarmac crossroads. Turn right and follow the sign for Duncton, which shortly brings you back to Burton Mill.

Walk 24: Petworth, Upperton and Tillington

This walk is not particularly long, but you can stretch it to fill whatever time you have available by exploring Petworth Park – a most relaxing and enjoyable excursion.

Starting Point: Petworth town car park, just south of the market square. GR 977216. Map: OS Explorer 133.

Distance: 4 – 5 miles

Terrain: Gently undulating

Local Information: There are toilets near to the entrance to the car park.

The Churches

Petworth, Sacred Heart: This church was founded by an enthusiastic Catholic, Charles Dawes of Burton Hill, in 1896. The architect of this large, curvilinear building with a fine apse was Frederick A. Walters.

Sacred Heart RC church, Petworth

Petworth, St Mary the Virgin: Picturesque Lombard Street leads from Market Square up to the church. The tall, box-like tower can be seen from the countryside around Petworth. A steeple is missing. That designed by Charles Barry (Houses of Parliament architect) failed. The base of the tower is medieval. The chancel is 13th-century, the north arcade 14th-century. Little remains of a Saxon church mentioned in Domesday, but here is a complex, historic building.

Tillington, All Hallows: A church was first built here, above the River Rother in the Forest of the Weald, in 1180. The oldest parts of this building are the nave and south arcade: they and the font are Transition-

Norman. The chancel was restored between 1807 and 1837 in Early English style. The 13th-century chancel arch escaped this restoration. The most dramatic change of 1807 was the removal of the tower and its replacement with a taller one with a Scots Crown on top. This is the most southerly Scots Crown in Britain. The third Lord Egremont of Petworth House is responsible for this tower. Despite criticism of it, this church has been the subject of paintings by both Turner and Constable.

Tillington church

The Walk

From the toilets near the entrance to the car park, set off up the alley next to Rosemary Gardens. The alley opens into Rosemary Lane. At the T-junction with Grove Street turn left. Opposite Stone House, go through a gate on to a private road which leads to residential Sheep-down Drive. Turn left here and again at the main road, Angel Street. Diagonally opposite is the Catholic church.

From the Catholic church, follow the adjacent lane down past ecclesiastical buildings to a footpath which skirts east Petworth. It overlooks meadows and streams of the delightful valley, the Shimmings. Turn left on to this path and follow it north to the first cross-paths at Barton Lane. Turn left up a lane which brings you opposite the parish church of Petworth. Under the 20th-century tower is an ancient building.

To enter Petworth Park you have to run the gauntlet of traffic on the busy A272, north out of Petworth. From the parish church, turn left and hug walls at the edge of Petworth House for 100 metres, until you can escape into Cow Yard on the left. Follow signs to the pedestrian tunnel which takes you under the 'Pleasure Grounds'. Heave a sigh of relief when you emerge in Petworth Park with its magnificent hill, sparkling lake and diverse wildlife. You can wander freely in the 400 hectares (2000 acres) of park. This is a beautiful place of illusions; the 'natural' landscape has been cleverly adapted by Capability Brown from bogs and planted with clumps of beeches, oaks and chestnuts. Large herds of fallow deer are descendants of the 72 introduced in Elizabethan times. All seems wild and free, but try to enter or leave and a 14-mile, massive stone wall is in the way. Follow the next instructions for a secret exit!

From the tunnel, walk down to the lake or 'Upper Pond'. Petworth House, with its 63 windows, is behind you. Keep to the left of the lake and you join a gravel track heading west towards Tillington. Where the track branches, veer right and gently uphill with Tillington Church, hidden in summer, away on your left and rural views on your right. No short cuts to Tillington – the park wall is impregnable! Instead, keep to the track as it leads uphill north-west and gently down. In the valley turn left off the track. Climb a slope with spring water on your right. Two gates take you out of the park at Upperton. This village is set on a sandstone ridge way above the River Rother.

At Upperton, turn left down the road to Tillington. The park wall is on the left and you pass a sports field on the right. Below can be seen the distinctive Scots Crown of Tillington Church, and in the distance the

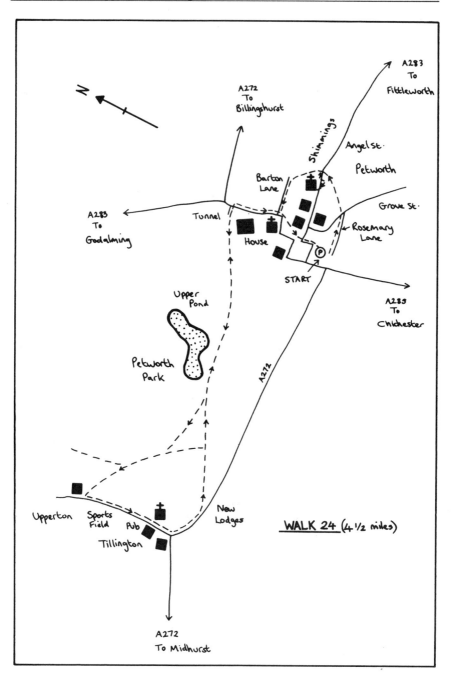

N

A283
To
Fittleworth

A272
To
Billingshurst

Shimmings

Angel St.

Petworth

A283
To
Godalming

Tunnel

Barton
Lane

Grove St.

Rosemary
Lane

House

P

START

A283
To
Chichester

Upper
Pond

Petworth
Park

A272

Upperton

Sports
Field

Pub

Tillington

New
Lodges

WALK 24 (4½ miles)

A272
To Midhurst

real country. Opposite the church are the village stores and pub. Behind the pub is a lane leading to Tillington Manor. We return to the church.

After visiting the church, stay in the churchyard and find the footpath in the east corner. This leads to the A272 Petworth to Midhurst road. Keep the wall on the left and after 400 metres re-enter Petworth Park at the New Lodges. Back inside the park, make for Petworth House with its ancient chapel. Retrace your steps through the tunnel and back to the parish church. Opposite the church is the narrow, cobbled lane, Lombard Street. This leads south via Market Square and the shopping arcade to the car park.

Walk 25: Fittleworth, Egdean and Stopham

Fine views, peaceful countryside, historic buildings and a church with evidence of its 11th-century origins make this a truly memorable walk.

Starting Point: Fittleworth Church, at the north end of the village. GR 009193. This walk crosses three Explorer Maps. The recommended OS Landranger Map 197 covers all the terrain.

Distance: 8 miles

Terrain: Gently undulating

The Churches

Fittleworth, St Mary: Early English in style, as the lancet windows testify, but the Victorians changed the nave and aisles and put unusual dormer windows in the roof. The 13th-century tower has a broach spire.

Egdean, St Bartholomew: Few houses are left in this quiet corner. The church was rebuilt in 1622 of stone rubble and brick. It was restored in the 19th century, apart from one window in the west wall. The doorway and its brick arch are 17th century. The bellcote and porch are later additions.

Stopham, St Mary the Blessed Virgin: Nineteen inhabitants of Stopham are mentioned in Domesday: Ralph, Robert, Torquil and 16 villeins. The church was built some time around 1066. A small, blocked window in the north wall of the chancel, the shapely south doorway and the original high arches above the north and south doorways are of this period. The chancel arch and parts of the tower are Norman. The other windows in the chancel are Early English. Two local families who came over with William the Conqueror and have stayed ever since are commemorated in this church. They are the Barttelot family from the Manor and de Stopham family from Stopham House.

The Walk

From Fittleworth Church cross the road to the track, heading south-west over Hesworth Common. At cross paths take the middle path, then fork right. Soon you reach a sandy mound with fine views south to the Downs. Go down steps and continue south-west through well-spaced trees and, in summer, bracken. At a lane turn left down to a small cluster of houses including Hesworth Farm.

Turn right here and go west across open fields. You emerge through a gate on to Woodruff Lane. Opposite is a converted barn with a lovely garden gathered around a natural pond. Turn right up the lane, which leads to a main road. Cross to the lane opposite and Egdean Church is ahead, up a lane to the left.

Before you reach Egdean Church you pass a footpath on your right. Return to this path to continue the walk. It leads north through a wooded lane next to the A283. At a finger post at the top of the lane, turn right through a gap in the woodland, there is a path east. The fingerpost does not acknowledge this but it is confirmed when you cross the A283. You enter a field through a gap next to a metal gate. Walk east along a rough track for over 200 metres.

At a rickety gate on the right, tumble down into a wide, open field. Hug woodland on the left as you continue east to the houses of Little Bognor, a quiet hamlet with lovely gardens. At the tarmac lane through this hamlet, turn left, and after 100 metres turn right to a footpath which flanks the lowest edge of a fine millstream garden. This path goes east with fine views on the right over rolling fields to the Downs. Ancient Fitzleroi Farm is ahead just to the right.

At the tarmac road, turn right as if to the farm then fork away left along a slender, open lane. Pass Amen Cottage on your right then climb to another road, which you cross diagonally south-east to a path opposite. This goes through woodland and can be very muddy, especially in winter. In half a mile you reach a track at Churchwood with a bungalow on the left. Head south down the track, passing scattered houses and hedged gardens. The track curves then emerges on to a lane. Cross to a footpath which is well hidden by trees and shrubs. It is immediately opposite a private driveway. Climb through undergrowth, heading south-east to the main A283, Petworth to Pulborough road.

At a gate to the A283, veer away left to a sandy path up through trees. Some wooden steps have been provided and lead through bracken. The path curves right to join a well-defined track leading to Stopham. As you reach the village, Stopham Manor, a stone, probably 17th-century house is opposite. Turn right for the village green and Stopham Church.

From the church, retrace your steps to the track opposite the Manor House. Do not follow the track. Instead, turn left down a lane which

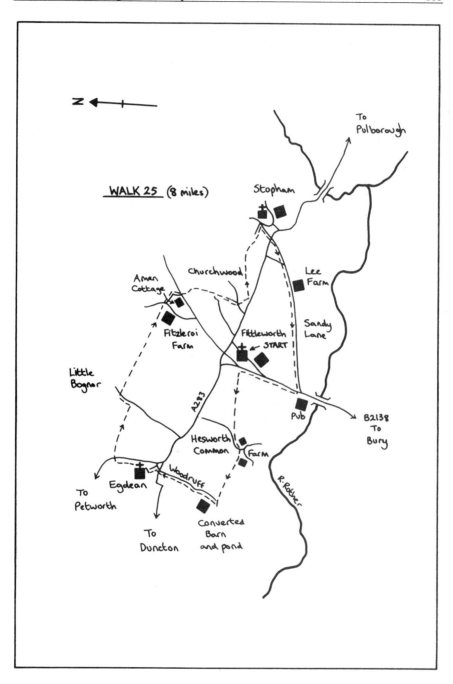

WALK 25 (8 miles)

Stopham church

leads south-west to the main road. Cross to Sandy Lane opposite and this will take you back to Fittleworth. There are fine views south to water meadows and the River Rother. Lee Farm, a fine Elizabethan building, has a commanding position over the Rother. At Fittleworth you emerge on the main road to Bury, also the village street. Turn right and you pass the village shop. At the first road junction, fork left. At the second road junction, fork right. Fittleworth Church is on the right.

Walk 26: Fernhurst and Lurgashall

If you do not mind one muddy climb, this is a wonderful walk. In May, with the bluebells and blossom, nowhere is more beautiful. There is even a chance to sample locally produced wine (or coffee) en route!

Starting Point: Fernhurst car park, west of the A286 Midhurst to Haslemere road, near crossroads in Fernhurst. GR 899285. Map: OS Explorer 133.

Distance: 7 or 8 miles

Terrain: One long hill, some mud.

The Churches

Fernhurst, St Mary of Antioch: The church is near the village green. It was successfully restored by Anthony Salvin in 1881. The tower is completely of this period. Remnants of the original 12th-century church are in the stone rubble walls. Also Norman are the small window in the north wall of the nave and the thin buttress outside the north wall. Fernhurst has been a thriving village at the centre of the Wealden iron works, and it has cared for its church. Today's villagers have contributed lovely, colourful kneelers with scenes of wild life in tapestry.

Lurgashall, St Laurence: Also near the village green, you enter this church through a timber gallery which was a meeting and resting place for parishioners in the 16th century. In 1622 it was enclosed to make a village school. Inside this gallery is a Resurrection Stone to put on graves to protect them from the hands of dissectors. There is also an early font, broken by Puritans. It has the marks of the lock used to prevent holy water from being stolen. The font inside the church is of Sussex marble and dates from 1662. The nave is large with some Saxon work in the north and south walls. The chancel is Early English with a Norman arch. The tower arch is also Norman. The tower itself, first built in 13th century, has been renewed over the ages. Tennyson lived at Aldworth House on Black Down and came to worship in this church.

The Walk

To begin this dream walk from the car park, cross the A286 and walk down the lane opposite. You are heading east past Fernhurst Church to the village green. Cross the green to a footpath next to the pub. You are

Fernhurst church

soon in a bluebell wood cut by streams. People have wandered around, creating new paths, but the public right of way is well defined.

At a T-junction with a woodman's track, turn left and follow the track. In 100 metres ignore the left fork and keep climbing north-east, in the bed of a stream through Reeth Copse. This is the muddy bit. Eventually you reach a lone house, Reeths, on your right. Turn right on a firm track. There are fine views south over Fernhurst Research Station to Bexleyhill with its dominant mast.

Walk east along this track to Fernden Lane. This skirts Blackdown, the highest hill in Sussex. There is a path to the top diagonally opposite as you emerge on to the lane. For our walk today, turn right along Fernden Lane for about 100 metres. Take the first footpath right into Blackdown Park. Blackdown House is said to have been the hunting lodge of Oliver Cromwell.

Go downhill in a south-easterly direction towards the cottages of Blackdown Farm, which you pass on the left, and a lake on the right. Keep gently down through a newly planted avenue to Ewhurst Lodge (1901) with the motto 'Fide non Perfide'. Next is Windfallwood. Continue on the path through the wood for 100 metres to Jobson's Lane.

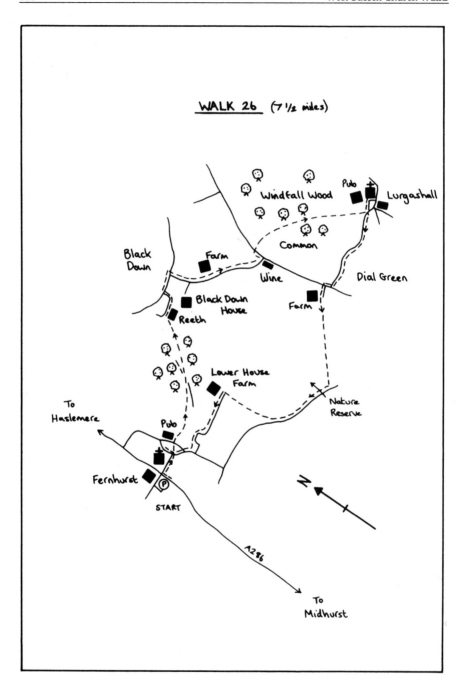

WALK 26 (7 ½ miles)

Windfall Wood

Pub

Lurgashall

Black Down

Farm

Common

Wine

Dial Green

Black Down House

Farm

Reeth

Lower House Farm

To Haslemere

Pub

Nature Reserve

Fernhurst

P

START

A286

To Midhurst

N

Lurgashall Winery is on the right. Coffee is served here and you can also taste the home-made wine.

For the walk! At Jobson's Lane turn left away from the winery, then turn right up a lane past Guardian Cottage. Follow the lane as it curves left past a work store to a wood, known as Windfallwood Common. There are two paths into the wood. Take the narrower path on the left. This takes you up through a strip of wild woodland where your way is strewn with wood anemones and bluebells in the spring. Reluctantly, you leave the wood for further delights: apple orchards are in blossom below and the steeple of Lurgashall Church beckons.

Pass a bungalow on your right and turn left at a lane which draws you to the quintessential relaxed village green. Pass Noah's Ark, the pub on your left, and the way to the church grave meadow is slumbering under patches of wild flowers, garlic and nettles. Return to the green, pass the post office and shop and turn right along a road signed to Haslemere. This brings you back to the bungalow. Instead of the footpath, take the tarmac lane and keep on it for over half a mile to the T-junction at Dial Green.

Turn right here, and in a few metres left. This path goes beside a lake and past farm cottages of Great Brockhurst Farm. There are views up to Blackdown on the right. Keep heading west for nearly a mile and ignore paths on the right. At a tarmac road turn right, pass a nature reserve and footpath on the right. Take the second path. It has a hidden sign, 'Lower House Farm, Private'. This is Stroud Lane Path and leads to a beautiful lake, home of Canada geese. On the other side stands the fine, old farmhouse. Keep up the lane and turn left at T-junction along a driveway in front of the farmhouse.

This driveway leads to houses on the edge of Fernhurst. Pass Pear Tree Cottage and continue on a tarmac path through Fernhurst Bottom to the village green and church. Cross the A286 back to the car park. The dream is over!

Walk 27: Northchapel, Ebernoe and Ebernoe Common

This walk is not particularly long or arduous, but it is very rewarding. The two Victorian churches are quite distinctive, and walking in Ebernoe Common is a pleasure at any time of year.

Starting Point: Northchapel Village Hall, on the road to Balls Cross. GR 954295. Map: OS Explorer 133.

Distance: 5 – 6 miles

Terrain: Fairly flat

The Churches

Northchapel

Northchapel, St John the Baptist: This is a pleasant Victorian church in Early English style. The font dates back to1662. Every church has some treasure and this one has a rare stained glass window depicting St Francis. It is the work of Wilhelmena Geddes.

Ebernoe, Holy Trinity: This is a very different Victorian church. It is built of red and yellow bricks made in the local kiln. Sadly, the kiln has closed. The windows are clear and look out on the woodland of Ebernoe Common, with its wild flowers and protected natural habitat of shy birds.

The Walk

From the village hall, walk east on the quiet, single track road towards Balls Cross. Take the third footpath to the right. It passes just behind the fine building of Peacocks Farm and in front of the farm cottage. From these idyllic houses, it is a shock to see ahead a 'flying saucer' resting on Beacon Hill. This is the Air Navigational Radio Beacon. At least we have the benefit of its firm track for 300 metres, before bearing right into woodland.

Inside the wood, at a cross-paths, turn left down through fir trees. In the summer there should be foxgloves bordering the path. This curves left out of the wood and down a well-drained field to a copse, Mercers Furze. You hug this on your right. On your left across the field, Freehold

Ebernoe church

Farm and barns stand exposed. Cross the farm road and continue straight on until the path turns left. You cross a field to a wooded dell, complete with babbling brook!. This is a foretaste of Ebernoe Common.

After crossing a wooden footbridge, climb through silver birch, oaks and holly, bracken and bluebells to beech trees. Ignore the path to the right. Keep straight on past large ponds on the left and the garden walls of Ebernoe House on the right. Turn left at Ebernoe Lane and cross diagonally to a short path through woodland to the church. The furnace pond is behind the church in the wild life reserve of Ebernoe Common.

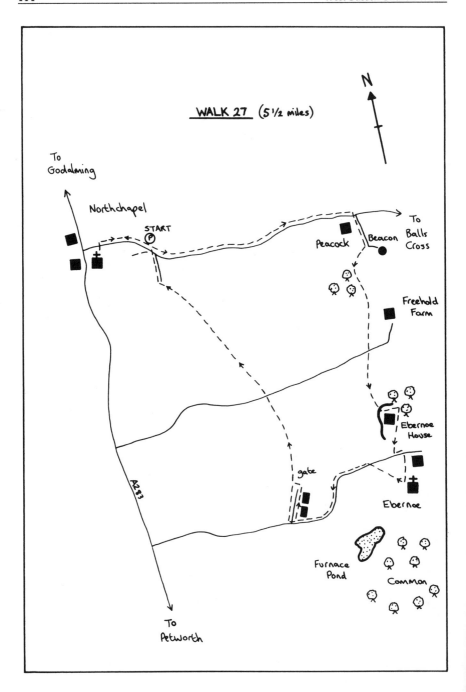

WALK 27 (5½ miles)

N

To
Godalming

Northchapel

START
ⓟ

To Balls Cross

Peacock

Beacon

Freehold Farm

Ebernoe House

gate

A283

Ebernoe

Furnace Pond

Common

To
Petworth

To walk back to Northchapel, return to the gate where you entered the churchyard, turn left and follow another path back to Ebernoe Lane. Turn left here and follow the lane for half a mile. After two bends you reach a farm building and track on the right. Turn up here and head north past a few cottages. At a gate at the end of the track, turn left. In 100 metres turn right and continue north through a tree-lined grass or mud way.

After crossing a farm lane, the path veers north-west for half a mile – ignore turnings to left and right. After you emerge from the wood, Northchapel Church can be seen ahead on the left. At Hortons Farm you rejoin the road to Balls Cross. Turn left and the village hall is on the right. To visit the church, keep straight on to the main A283, turn left and the church is on the left.

Walk 28: Kirdford and Wisborough Green

Some of this walk is on tarmac lanes, but it still offers much pleasant walking through woodland and along farm tracks. The churches are particularly interesting, both architecturally and historically.

Starting Point: Kirdford Church GR 018265. Map: OS Explorer 134.

Distance: 8 miles

Terrain: Mainly flat

The Churches

Kirdford, St John the Baptist: This large church, to the south-east of the village and opposite a pub, has the largest parish in West Sussex. Kirdford has traditionally been a centre of industry. Until 1880 Sussex marble was quarried here. The font and paving slabs of the church porch are of Sussex marble. Glass has been made in local furnaces. The lancet window in the north aisle has fragments of glass collected by a local apple farmer. There are apple orchards in Kirdford still. The Norman origins of the church survive in the blocked south doorway and some herringbone work in the masonry of the south and west walls. The spa-

Kirdford church

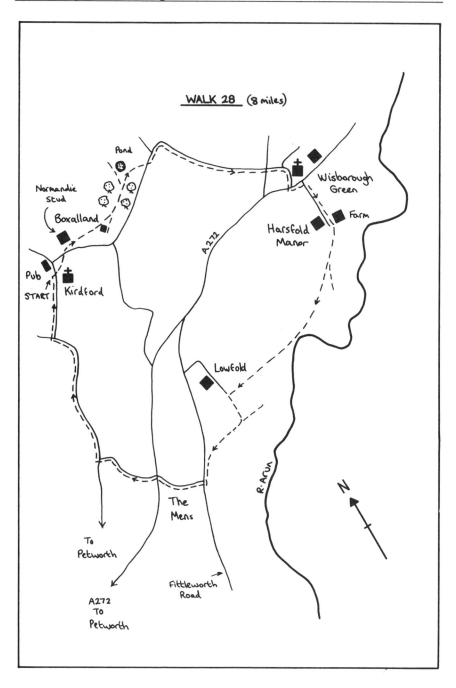

WALK 28 (8 miles)

Pond

Normandie Stud

Boxalland

Wisborough Green

Farm

Harsfold Manor

A272

Pub
START
Kirdford

Lowfold

R. Arun

N

The Mens

To Petworth

Fittleworth Road

A272 TO Petworth

cious north aisle is 13th century. The chancel was rebuilt in the 14th or 15th century with squints on either side. The chancel arch is modern. The tower, in three storeys, was added in the 15th century.

Wisborough Green, St Peter Ad Vincula: This church has a commanding position on a hill near the River Arun. It was probably used by the Normans as a fortress to guard this important waterway – the walls are over 4ft thick. The church was first mentioned in 1227, when Henry III allowed a yearly fair at 'Wyseberg'. The north and south doors of the Norman nave are high enough for horsemen to pass through. The elegant Early English chancel still has its original stone altar, hidden by villagers during the Reformation and returned to Wisborough Green in 1901. The medieval wall painting shows Christ crucified between thieves. The imposing 14th-century spire was saved from fire in 1857 by George Smith, the village constable. After a thunderstorm, which brought down the cross and set the spire alight, he climbed the tower and put out the flames.

The Walk

From Kirdford Church, turn right and walk through the churchyard to a gate, behind the church. Cross the sports field to the road to Wisborough Green. Turn right along the road for 50 metres. At Normandie Stud, turn left and walk between green-painted, corrugated buildings, then through an avenue. Follow the path to the right as it curves through woods. Pass the cottage and turn left at a T-junction of paths. Walk through the woodland, ignoring the path to the left. At a pond, turn right. Keep on your path – it rejoins the Wisborough Green Road. Turn left on to this road and follow it for over half a mile as it curves south to Wisborough Green.

The church is past the green, high on the left. Pass in front of the church, go through the churchyard and back to the main road. Opposite is a lane down to the River Arun. Cross over and walk down this lane. Harsfold Manor is on your right. Keep straight on along a narrow footpath. Turn right where the paths diverge. From this path you can look across the narrow River Arun eventually to meadows and hills opposite. Cross through fields, with Lowfold Farm on your right. Turn left at a farm track, away from Lowfold.

At a T-junction of farm tracks, turn right up to Fittleworth Road where there is a scattering of houses. Turn left on to this road and proceed for 200 metres, then turn right up a tarmac lane marked to Kirdford. This curves north-west through the ancient forest, the Mens. Cross the A272 and continue up the lane opposite. Keep to the tarmac lanes. At a T-junction, turn right along a lane with hedges and views on the left over to Black Down. Kirdford is about 1 mile ahead.

Walk 29: Eartham and Boxgrove

This is a gentle walk from a modest village church to a celebrated, former Benedictine priory. A short detour is possible to visit the windmill on Halnaker Hill.

Starting Point: Thicket Lane, Eartham, a quarter mile south of the church. GR 927084. Map: OS Explorer 121.

Distance: 6 miles (plus half a mile to visit the windmill)

Terrain: Undulating

The Churches

Eartham, St Margaret: Eartham is a small village on the south side of the Downs. The little church is unobtrusively in the centre of the village, next to Eartham House, now a school. The Norman origins of the church can be seen in the tall north doorway and large chancel arch.

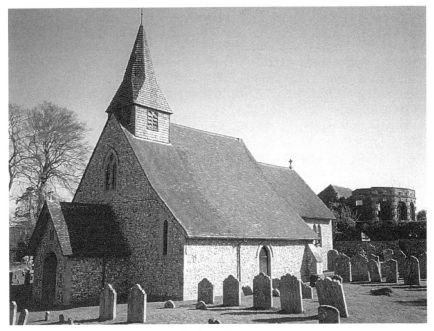

Earthem church

One of the carvings of the arch capital is of a hare's head. In the 13th century the chancel arch was rebuilt and a south aisle was added. Victorians, who restored the church in 1869, were content to keep it simple and compact.

Arch capital carving in Eartham church

Boxgrove Priory Church, St Mary and St Blaise: At the dissolution of the priory, the church was given to the parish. It is a magnificent church with the best of Norman and Early English styles. The great Norman pillars stand side by side with fluted Early English columns. The chancel is entirely Early English with three tall lancets in the east window. The church is cruciform. The north transept was the entrance to services for the monks. The south transept houses the de la Warr chapel, built in 1532 and with elaborate carving. There are beautiful foliage paintings in the vaulted roof.

The Walk

Thicket Lane stretches east to west for about half a mile before bending north. At the south corner of this bend is a footpath through gravel works. Head south down this path and in under half a mile you reach Tinwood Lane. Turn right here with the works on your right. Go through woodland and take the first path off to the left over flat, open country. It is a wide path with newly-planted trees. Boxgrove Priory can be seen ahead.

In order to enter Boxgrove Church, you have to pass the priory ruins and reach the south side. So, at a T-junction, turn left on a path which passes the priory to your right. Take the first path right and this brings you to the little lane which gives access to the church. There are fine, old cottages in this lane and the post office and stores are at the end, across the village street. Mind the cars!

After visiting Boxgrove Church, retrace your steps on the footpaths east then north so that the priory is now on your left. These paths, grassy and tree-lined, are a credit to the Council and all who have made them pleasant walking terrain. Instead of taking the path on the right which brought you here, keep straight on, heading north. Ignore a path to the left. Our path soon curves left and in 100 metres you turn right, behind Halnaker village. Go north-east and cross Tinwood Lane diagonally to the right, to a footpath which continues in the same direction,

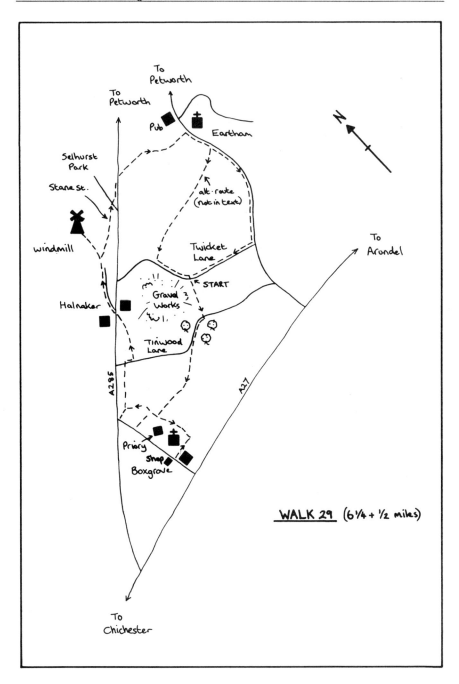

To Petworth

To Petworth

Pub

Eartham

Selhurst Park

Stane St.

alt·route (not in text)

windmill

Twicket Lane

To Arundel

START

Halnaker

Gravel Works

Tinwood Lane

A285

A27

Priory

Shop

Boxgrove

WALK 29 (6¼ + ½ miles)

To Chichester

up across a field. At the far side go through a gap in some trees. You have another field to cross, heading due north to the A285, Chichester to Pet-worth road.

Cross the A285 to a farm entrance opposite, then turn up a lane on your right which leads to Halnaker Hill and the windmill. You pass lovely, old Sussex cottages at the lower end of the lane. You are now in Stane Street, the Roman road from Chichester to the top of Bignor Hill and on to London. After the second gate, you can see the windmill to the left and Stane Street to the right. Visit the windmill and return to follow Stane Street. This goes through scrubland with two steep stiles. Your ef-fort is rewarded when you soon reach open fields, clumps of trees and views to Selhurst Park ahead. Go down the field path to the A285 at a lay-by.

At the A285, turn left for 100 metres past the private road to Selhurst Park on the left and cross the main road to a footpath diagonally oppo-site. This leads up through a copse to Long Down. From the top of Long Down you can see the village of Eartham ahead, below you. The path down is flanked by the remnants of a fir tree avenue. You reach Eartham immediately opposite the church. The pub is 100 metres up on the left.

From the church, turn south and down the tarmac road for nearly half a mile, until you come to the turning on the right, Thicket Lane.

Walk 30: Upwaltham, East Dean and the South Downs Way

We have walked this route in the snow, with blue skies, sunshine, bracing winds, brilliant fields and trees half dressed in white. It was a good test of the suitability of paths and, apart from the South Downs Way, which was frozen slippery, they were all excellent.

Starting Point: Upwaltham Church, west of the A285 and opposite Upwaltham Farm. GR 943138. Map: Explorer 121.

Distance: 8 miles

Terrain: Hilly

The Churches

Upwaltham, St Mary the Virgin: 'The Hills ... Upwaltham Church, the Downs seem to me only less beautiful than Heaven,' wrote Cardinal Manning last century. He speaks for the many who must have delighted in this building since its origins in 12th century. There were more trees on the slopes then: the name 'Upwaltham' means home or enclosure in the forest. The church has remained basically the same shape since it was built. It has a beautifully curved or apsidal chancel and the walls are both high and sturdy, made with flint and stone, almost a metre thick. The font is as ancient as the church. The south doorway was re-built in the 14th century. The fine chancel arch is Early English, as are the chancel windows with trefoil heads. The glass is clear and you look through to the beautiful Downs.

East Dean, All Saints: Built in the shape of a cross, the church is quite plain inside and much loved by the villagers of East Dean, including the poet Christopher Fry. The church is close to the village and yet on a slope of the Downs away from it all. First mentioned in 689, East Dean probably had a wooden church. King Alfred almost certainly came here, and as a devout monarch would have seen that the village had a church. The oldest parts of the existing building are the tower, transept and chancel, all built about 1150. The rest of the church is mainly Early English – the south doorway and lancet windows, for example.

Upwaltham

The Walk

A small, square, flint well house opposite Upwaltham Farm is at the base of a track up to the church. After visiting the church, return to the A285 and turn right. In 200 metres turn right on to a footpath up Waltham Down, going north-west. As you climb you see, down on the right, the cluster of buildings which form Upwaltham. There have never been many people living here. Ahead on the left are two clumps of trees; on the right, woodland. Follow the edge of the woodland for about 1 mile as it curves north. Find the way into Charlton Forest ahead.

Inside Charlton Forest, turn left on a well-defined track heading south-west. Avoid all turnings to left and right and keep on the straight, wide forest track. After 1 mile this veers south downhill and soon becomes a pretty, tree-lined lane perched above a valley, with glimpses across to Newhouse Farm and New Barn on the right. Go down the lane for half a mile then turn right across a field. East Dean can be seen ahead on the left. At a farm lane turn left. The church is 100 metres on the right.

The pub is below in the village and not far away. But to return to Upwaltham, retrace your steps from the church back to the farm lane. Instead of turning right along the footpath which brought you here, keep on the lane north in a wide valley. Pass New Barn and then the hand-

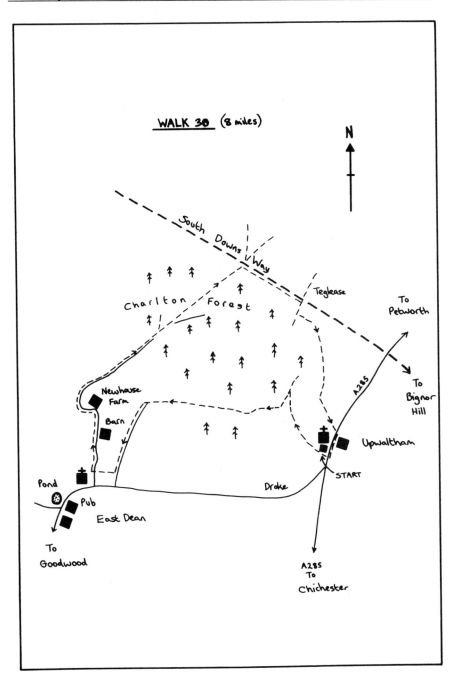

WALK 30 (8 miles)

some Newhouse Farm, where the road makes a wide curve west before settling to a north-east course. Twentieth century civilization gives way as the road enters a huge, bumpy arena in Charlton Forest. The bumps or ridges are a medieval field system or 'lynchets'.

Keep north-east, take the second footpath to the left, ignoring the left footpath. Pass the lynchets on your left and climb steadily to the edge of Charlton Forest. I believe this is the largest forest in the South of England. Admire the view behind then plunge boldly into the forest. The footpath follows a clearly defined track north-east and uphill for over 1 mile. Do not deviate onto any cross tracks. As you approach the South Downs Way, the forest recedes on your right. The South Downs Way runs along the top of Charlton Forest so, if you keep uphill, you are bound to reach it.

At the South Downs Way a signpost points to East Dean, Cocking, Graffham, Lavington and, for us, Upwaltham. Turn right along the South Downs Way, which gently rides the Downs from west to east. The ground is stony. Climb up to the highest point, Teglease signpost, with magnificent views north, and turn right into the forest again. In 75 metres turn left and south-east through bluebell woods. In under half a mile emerge from woodland to view over to Bignor Hill with two masts. The path turns right then left down a long slope to Upwaltham Church.

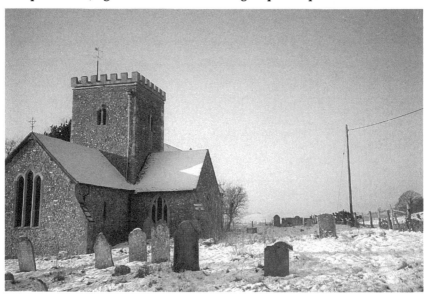

East Dean

10 Walks
near
Arundel

Arundel Cathedral

Walk 31: Arundel, South Stoke, North Stoke and Burpham

There is an early option to drastically reduce this walk – I recommend that you ignore it! The churches on this walk are impressive, interesting and inspiring; the views are magnificent; and Arundel is worthy of a leisurely exploration – why would you want to miss any of it?

Starting Point: The town entrance to Arundel Park, in a lane beyond the cathedral, on the other side of London Road. GR 013074. Map: OS Explorer 121.

Distance: 10 miles

Terrain: Hilly

The Churches

Arundel, St Nicholas: The church's long and eventful history reflects the importance of this medieval port on the River Arun. There was a church here in Saxon times, mentioned in Domesday. It fell into disrepair when the Plague depleted the population in 1349. Richard, Earl of Arundel had the church rebuilt in 1380. He kept the east end as a chapel for his college of secular priests. The large, wrought iron screen separating the chapel from the parish church is here still. In 1544, when Henry V111 sold the chapel and college, the west end continued as a parish church. The east end, the Fitzalan Chapel, fell into disrepair. In 1644 Roundheads used it to stable horses, and put canons on top of the tower to bombard the castle. In the 19th century the chapel was sold back to the Duke Of Norfolk and restored for Roman Catholic services. After a period of squabbling and erecting walls, in 1977 a joint service was held here with the screen open. It is now possible to go behind the altar of the parish church and look through the ancient grille to the beautiful Fitzalan Chapel. The style of the church throughout is Perpendicular. It retains many treasures from 1380, including a unique stone pulpit, frescoes and a font of Sussex marble.

Arundel Cathedral of Our Lady and St Philip Howard: Arundel Cathedral and Castle together dominate the town and the countryside around. They stand on the hill which rises from the river to the Downs. Under the patronage of Henry, 15th Duke of Norfolk, the church of St

Philip Neri was built of Bath stone between 1870-1873 at a cost of £70,000. The architect was Aloysius Hansom, who invented the Hansom cab. He chose the French Gothic style of 1300. In 1965 the church became a cathedral with a new patron, St Philip Howard, 13th Earl of Arundel. He had refused to give up the Catholic faith and was locked in the Tower of London by Queen Elizabeth the first. He died there eleven years later in 1595, aged 39.

South Stoke, St Leonard: Entwined in the River Arun, South Stoke Church is enchanting. Successive ages have contributed to this effect. The Saxons made the basic shape: simple chancel and nave. The Normans added the doorways. The 13th century contributed the vaulted porch and lancet windows in the west of the nave. The slender tower is

South Stoke, St Leonard

also 13th century. The 19th century added the charming, chateau-like spire with dormer windows. At the same time the inside of the church was swept clean and the chancel arch in crisp, white chalk added. This is in contrast with the rugged flint exterior. Greatest of all favours, the 20th century has passed by this church, not even installing electricity.

North Stoke: Although at the end of a farm track, this church is not forgotten. The Churches' Conservation Trust has cared lovingly for this building. It is a delight to enter the lofty nave and imbibe the spirit of ages past. The nave was probably built over a small, wooden Saxon church mentioned in Domesday. This church, in the shape of a cross, is mainly 13th century with six styles of window from 1200 to 1270. The small lancet high in the south wall of the nave is the oldest (1200). A 14th-century painting shows faintly on the wall above the richly moulded, horseshoe chancel arch.

Burpham, St Mary: Burpham was one of a string of hill forts set up by King Alfred (871-899) to keep out the Danes. The church is high on the northern edge of the village. Originally Saxon, it was remodelled at the end of the 12th century with a cruciform shape. The nave, ornate south transept arch and plain north transept arch are Norman. The chancel is 13th century. It has single lancet windows and a trefoil lancet with pointed arch of about 1340. The west tower is 15th century. In the churchyard a tombstone of 1789 has the carving of a racehorse with the jockey Benjamin Brewster.

The Walk

Off the London Road, on the opposite side to the cathedral, a fingerpost indicates the path up a quiet lane next to the walled grounds of the castle and towards Arundel Park. Walk into the park as far as Hiorne Tower. Turn right here and pass the tower on your left. Ahead, a post points the way straight on, down past young trees to your right. Turn left on to a track which descends gently north-east, passing Swanbourne Lake below on the right. Cross the valley to a path through a gate and head north up sloping downland to the tree plantation ahead. Behind are views to the coast. At the trees keep left and skirt the north tip of the plantation. At the top, a new vista opens over the River Arun and beyond. Keeping north, cross the open Downs to a gate and footpath 100 metres ahead and below.

The path descends with sharp bends to right and left. It goes steeply down until you leave Arundel Park through a wall at the bottom. Turn right through trees beside the River Arun. The path rises above the river and crosses fields to a farm at South Stoke. Pass Chapel Barn and meet the tarmac road back to Arundel. It is a quiet lane offering the option of shortening the walk. In any case you will want to visit South Stoke Church. Turn left at the tarmac road and the church is 50 metres ahead. Retrace your steps to shorten the walk.

To do the full walk, turn right when you leave the church and a path leads to the river, which you cross on a footbridge. Turn sharp left and head north-west through a swampy copse over a suspension bridge and up a water meadow to North Stoke. You come out at North Stoke Road,

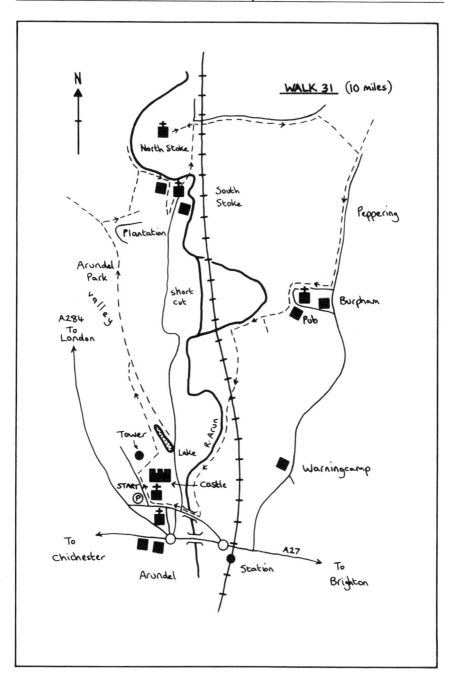

which will eventually take you up to Camp Hill. First, turn left down a farm lane and the church is at the end.

From the church, retrace your steps back to North Stoke Road. Head east up the road into the Downs. In one mile, high in remote downland, take the path off to the right. This path has a few bushes sheltering it. Turn right and south down the long track past Peppering High Barn to Burpham, one mile ahead. There are views to Arundel Castle and the sea in the distance. When you reach a tarmac road, turn right to Peppering Farm then left to Burpham Church.

From Burpham Church, head south past the pub, community hall and playing field. In the corner, near swings, there are footpaths, one to the left and our path straight ahead. It follows the escarpment above the River Arun for 50 metres, then descends to water meadows. Turn left and keep to the raised bank beside the river with tall rushes as a screen. Keep going for half a mile. Here the bank curves to the right; you take the track down left across a stream and over a field towards poplars. Ignore the path to the left and take the track south, passing the poplars on your right, then past the backs of gardens in Warningcamp.

At the tarmac lane turn right, cross the railway line and follow the river back to Arundel. When you arrive, cross the bridge into town. Continue up High Street, past the castle gates on your right, and you are in London Road, where Anglicans and Roman Catholics share the same building for their church. The cathedral looks askance from across the way.

Walk 32: Whiteways, Bury and Bignor

There are plenty of refreshment opportunities and other facilities on this route so it's a good idea to make it into a full day's outing by visiting Bignor Roman Villa.

Starting Point: The car park at Whiteways roundabout, at the junction of the A29, A289 and B2139. GR 002108. Map: OS Explorer 121.

Distance: 8 – 9 miles

Terrain: Hilly

Local Information: Whiteways has an outdoor snack bar and toilets.

The Churches

Bury, St John the Evangelist: The church is at the river end of the village: the 13th-century tower would have been a landmark for boatmen using this important waterway. A church at Burie is mentioned in Domesday (1087). Little remains of this building. The chancel was enlarged and given a new arch in the early-14th century. In 1855 it was again rebuilt. The south porch, with stoup or vessel for holy water, was added in the early 16th century. The roof has been raised and lowered. The rood beam is 13th century. The font and oak screen are 15th century.

Bignor, Holy Cross (formerly St Peter): The roads of Bignor form a square and the church is at the highest, north-west corner. You enter

Bignor church lych gate

the churchyard through the handsome, Victorian lych gate. The Victorians did much to restore this rapidly deteriorating church: the chancel roof had fallen in by 1743. It is a large building with north and south aisles and a generous porch. Bigeneure Church is mentioned in Domesday. The thick east wall of the nave and the plain, round chancel arch are built of large stones and are early Norman. Otherwise the church is Early English in style, with long lancet windows below a round window at the east end. The wooden screen dates back to 1320. The font is Norman on a modern base. The porch was rebuilt by the Victorians.

The Walk

From Whiteways, cross the busy A29, heading east. The fingerpost for this crossing is 50 metres outside the northern edge of the car park. The footpath down to Houghton is immediately opposite. It runs parallel to the B2139 and gives glimpses of magnificent scenery above the River Arun. You emerge from the hedge-lined footpath at the main road and pass the old inn, the George and Dragon, on the left. Turn left at the lane signed to Bury, with a black and white cottage on the corner. The South Downs Way crosses this lane. Turn right along the South Downs Way and then left along the riverbank to Bury. The church can be seen near the river.

After visiting the church, turn right up the village lane then right again up a private road. Ignore the path to the right; our footpath soon turns sharp left and takes you along the edge of a field to a T-junction of paths. Turn right here, up a track to the pub. From here cross to a track through cottages and down to the A29. The glass houses of a nursery are opposite. Cross and turn right down the service road and look for a footpath to the left. This leads into fields, which you cross diagonally towards a white farm track. A footbridge is just to the left of the track. Follow the fingerpost north-west across the field. After another footbridge you reach a junction of paths. Turn right and follow the edge of a copse, which you enter at an inward curve.

Inside the copse, after 100 metres, the path bends sharp right at a cottage and then comes to a little lane. Continue up the lane, go past Hale Hill Farm and you reach a small road. West Burton is to the left but we are going to Bignor along hidden tracks. Turn right and cross the road to a sunken way. Keep along this way for half a mile. On the right, peep through trees and over an escarpment to meadows below. Turn left at a fingerpost and head south towards the Downs. It is not yet time to climb back up. Instead, turn right along a path towards Hadworth Farm. Make

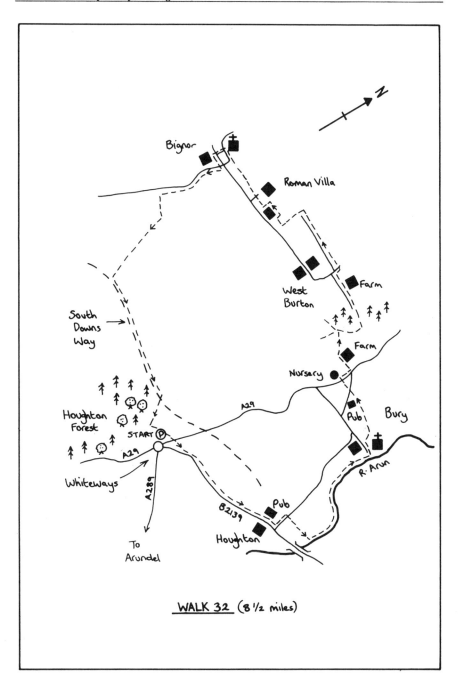

WALK 32 (8 ½ miles)

a detour of the farm and continue west towards Bignor Roman Villa (the snack bar is open in season). The village of Bignor is about 100 metres further on. On the left corner is an ancient cottage with a mixture of building styles. Turn right and follow the road through Manor Farm to the church.

From the church, head south down a village lane with pretty cottages. Pass two paths off to the right but do not turn until you reach Bignor Farmhouse with its lovely, well-tended garden. Turn right here up the tarmac road to Bignor Hill. After nearly half a mile uphill, turn left on to a bridleway which climbs through trees on a firm track (no longer the tarmac road!). At the top, keep straight on along the South Downs Way, heading south-east. There are extensive views over Houghton Forest to the coast. After 1 mile on the South Downs Way, turn right at a cross-paths at the corner of a wood and head south. Enter the wood and turn left along a woodland track which leads back to Whiteways. Another snack bar awaits you here.

Walk 33: Greatham Bridge, Hardham, Coldwaltham and Watersfield

This walk begins alongside a canal which was abandoned due to competition from the railways, and then follows the trackbed of the old Pulborough to Midhurst railway — now also abandoned!

Starting Point: Car park on the west side of Greatham Bridge. GR 031162. Map: OS Explorer 121.

Distance: 7 miles

Terrain: Fairly flat

Local Information: Greatham Bridge, south of Pulborough, was built between 1307 and 1327. It was the first and is the finest bridge over the River Arun.

The Churches

Hardham, St Botolph: A little, white church, standing back from the A29 just south of Pulborough, St Botolph's is dedicated to the patron saint of travellers Inside is a gallery of wall paintings, some of the oldest in England. The church building is 11th century, with a crude chancel arch which is Saxon in style. The walls are thick and of rugged Pulborough stone and some Roman material, maybe from the nearby Roman fort which served Stane Street. Medieval travellers along this Roman road, still a highway, would have rested at Hardham Church. There is a hermit's squint in the south wall of the chancel.

Coldwaltham, St Giles: This church is dedicated to the patron saint of the disabled. Stane Street is just north of Coldwaltham and travellers, especially the sick, would call here. The yew tree is one of the oldest at about 1000 years old,. The Norman tower, with its distinctive half-timbered top, is all that remains of the old building. The poor rural community had a struggle to keep the fabric intact and the Victorians rescued it from decay and added a north aisle and vestry. The windows are Decorated in style. Waltham was called 'Cold' in the 14th century, when floods came and surrounded the village. See *A Story Of Three Hamlets* by Sandra Saer for more details.

Watersfield Congregational Chapel: The chapel was modestly built of brick in 1823 and is close to Waltham Brooks Nature Reserve.

The Walk

From Greatham Bridge car park, turn left and in 100 metres, cross the road and head north, away from the river, on the Wey South Path. This follows the route of an old canal intended to link London with Portsmouth. When railways were built the canal could not compete and was abandoned. Now volunteers restore parts of the canal. This part of the path is lined with willows enjoying the boggy ground. The path itself is firm enough. On a bright day, with sunshine striking patches of lady's smock and sloe blossom, it is pretty. On a dull day it can be a gloomy tunnel. It does, in fact, lead to an extraordinary canal tunnel. Before we reach this, the path opens into a field and the remains of Hardham Priory can be spied on the right. Founded in 1234 for the black canons of St

Augustine, its few residents had a jolly time extorting food and ale and poaching in Bignor Park. Now it is in the grounds of a private house. The canal tunnel can be seen down on the right. It is barred by a metal grille. Our path veers left up a bank to road level. Pass a lone house and cross the main A29 to the footpath opposite.

This path crosses the railway line by a footbridge then zigzags north-east towards a large water works. Turn right at the works' road and walk over the level crossing back

Coldwaltham church

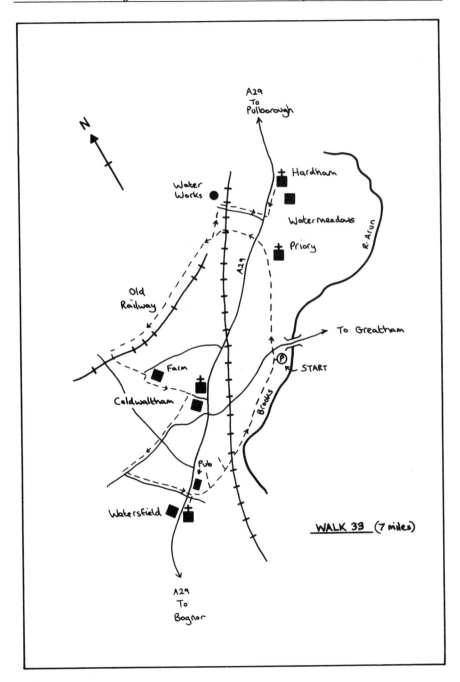

to the A29. Turn left along the road towards Pulborough. Hardham Church is 100 metres on the right in a lay-by. Inside, the walls are covered in paintings which have survived for nearly 900 years.

Retrace your steps back to the level crossing and water works' road, then back over the field towards the rail footbridge. Instead of crossing the footbridge, veer to the right along the track of the old Pulborough to Midhurst railway. The Countryside Commission has opened this to walkers. Follow the track west, with views on either side. To the right was the first resting place for Roman soldiers on Stane Street, and the River Rother is beyond. The River Arun and River Rother merge near the aqueduct which can be seen to the north-east. Our track continues west for 1 mile. At the end, turn sharp left into a hidden, narrow footpath which becomes wider and muddier. It soon emerges on a road to a farmhouse. Turn right through the farmhouse garden then left over a field and past bungalows. Head downhill, ignoring paths to left and right and Coldwaltham Church is on your left, near the A29.

From the church, retrace your steps for 100 metres, passing the village school on your right. Turn left up a sandy footpath on the boundary of Lodge Hill. This is now a study and activity centre. Formerly, it was the home of Arthur and Marion Paddon and known as Watersfield Towers. At the top the path opens on to a tarmac country road with scattered farms and cottages. Keep straight on along the road, past Coldwaltham Farm, then turn left towards Waltham Park Farm. This sandy lane takes you down to the main A29 at Watersfield. A pub is opposite and the chapel is on the same side, 100 metres south.

Take the lane south-east from the pub. At the bottom take the footpath on the left then turn right. Cross the railway line and cross the bridge to a wide, grassy path raised above marsh and ponds. This takes you north-east, back to the car park at Greatham Bridge.

Walk 34: Amberley, The Wild Brooks and Greatham

This route is liable to flooding and so should be attempted only in dry weather. If conditions are right, however, it is a fascinating walk, offering the chance to see a diversity of unusual flora and fauna.

Starting Point: Amberley Church GR 030133. Map: OS Explorer 121.

Distance: 6 miles

Terrain: Mainly flat

The Churches

Amberley, St Michael: The name 'Amberley' means the meadow of Eanburg, or even the field of yellow buttercups. This field was given to St Wilfrid and was to become an important religious centre. A Norman church was built in 1100 by Bishop Luffa. The magnificent chancel arch may have been the work of the same masons who built Chichester Cathedral. The blocked north doorway and the font are also Norman. The nearby fortified house, Amberley Castle, was, until the 16th century, the retreat of bishops from people who resented their wealth and

Amberley church

power. The parish church has benefited from the proximity of the bishops. In 1230 Bishop Ralph Neville built the Early English chancel, the south aisle and added the tower, now big with buttresses. To accommodate his retinue, the chancel is as big as the nave. To the right of the chancel arch are 12th- and 13th-century wall paintings. The 14th-century south doorway has capitals with carved oak leaves, bryony and buttercups.

Greatham Church: A single-cell church and similar to Wiggonholt (see the next walk). It has unusual masonry with Roman brick, Pulborough sandstone and rubble. It has evidence of work from the 11th, 12th and 13th centuries. The bell turret was damaged in 1987 and is replaced by a spire. The porch is also modern. Soldiers killed at the Battle of Greatham Bridge were buried here.

The Walk

From Amberley Church, walk past the pottery in an old chapel on the right. Village roads here have beautiful cottages. Take the road to the left and at the bend turn down a slope left, leaving the snug houses behind. Suddenly you are in Wild Brooks, a wide, flat, usually soggy alluvial plain. Fortunately, no major drainage scheme has been allowed and wild life has benefited. There are 400 flowering plants and ferns, 16 species of dragonfly and many birds, including Bewick's swans, herons, snipe, lapwing and yellow wagtail. Cattle grazing seasonally help to keep the grass healthy and their dung promotes insect life.

Head north on a track through Wild Brooks for over 1 mile, passing ditches and very few trees. After a spinney you leave Wild Brooks by a wooden bridge. Make for the converted wooden barn slightly to the left. Pass the barn and then a farm. The path is rising steadily and winds towards the River Arun with glimpses down to ancient Greatham Bridge. For 100 metres the path goes beside the river. At Greatham Bridge, turn right and walk along the tarmac road for half a mile. Pass the turning to Amberley and Rackham on the right. Greatham hamlet is opposite. It has a manor house, farm and Saxon church.

From the church, return to the Amberley and Rackham turning and head south-east for half a mile along this tree-lined lane. Pass a farm gate on the right, and 100 metres on take the footpath to the right. This skirts the base of a hill at Rackham. At a cross-paths, turn right over a footbridge to a field at the edge of the Wild Brooks. Go through the grounds of Rackham Mill, now a private house. After a small wood, climb the sloping field up to the part of Amberley known as Cross Gates. Turn right and walk about 1 mile along the road to Amberley, passing one pub at Cross Gates and another in the village itself.

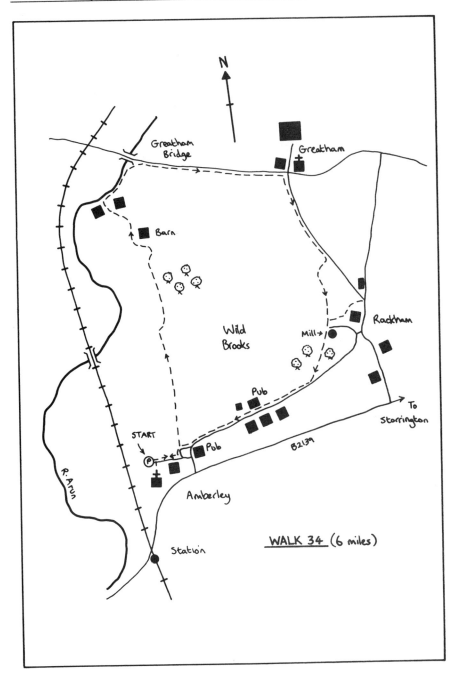

Walk 35: Rackham, Parham and Wiggonholt

Combine this walk with a visit to the RSPB Nature Reserve for a really interesting and varied day out.

Starting Point: Rackham Village Hall, north of the B2139, near Amberley. GR 050141. Map: OS Explorer 121.

Distance: 6 – 7 miles

Terrain: Some woodland but generally undemanding.

The Churches

Parham, St Peter: The church is tucked away to the south of the Elizabethan mansion, Parham House. The village of Parham has been destroyed. In 1778-9 the buildings were demolished and the people moved to Rackham. The church now stands here alone, facing the Downs. Little is left of the original stone building of 1148; just fragments in the walls of the chancel chapel. Henry V111 granted the manor of Parham to R. Palmer. He had the chancel chapel remodelled in 1545. The rest of the church was rebuilt between 1800 and 1820. The squire's pew with its own fireplace remains.

Wiggonholt Church: Here, the church looks out over a wide, flat plain down to the River Arun. Medieval shepherds who worked on this plain, the Brooks, came to shelter and worship in the church. It is still a remote place, with no houses apart from the two or three which form the hamlet of Wiggonholt. The church has no patron saint. It has a single room with stone rubble walls and was built in the 12th or 13th century. The roof has stone slabs and wooden beams inside. There is a Norman font of Sussex marble. The windows are Perpendicular, that is late 14th or 15th century. The quiet simplicity of this enduring church today draws walkers to shelter where once shepherds and their flocks rested.

The Walk

From the grassy space in front of Rackham Village Hall, head north, gently uphill along the tarmac lane. Pass Greatham Road on your left and turn right at West Lodges. This is the west driveway to beautiful

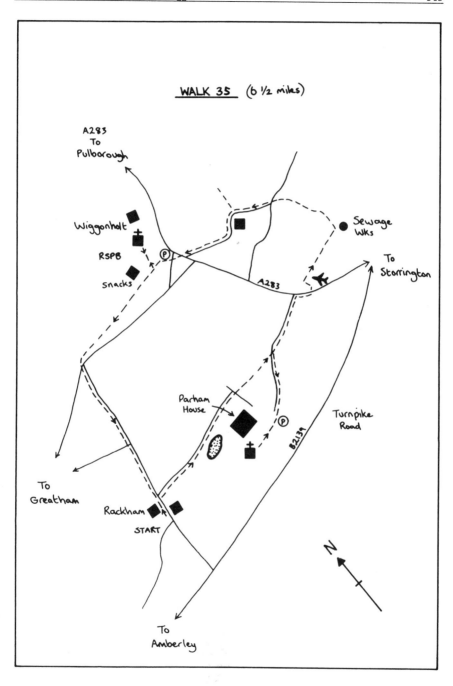

WALK 35 (6 ½ miles)

Parham House

Parham House, under half a mile ahead. First pass a lake on the right then the walls of the garden. At a crossways continue straight on towards the main driveway to Parham House. Turn sharp right here and follow the driveway back to the house. Go through the car park and past the south face of the house. The church is ahead, facing the Downs.

Return to the main driveway to entrance gates and emerge cautiously on to the A283, Pulborough to Storrington road. Diagonally opposite is a footpath around the edge of a private landing ground for small planes and gliders. When you have crossed the airstrip, you can see sewage works ahead. Turn left here across fields, heading gently uphill towards a copse. Continue through the copse to a tarmac lane. Turn left, then right and follow a farm track. This curves around Redford House and rises to the A283. Cross to Wiggonholt Common opposite. Turn right along an unofficial track which emerges at a minor road. Opposite, you will see a small car park. Enter the car park and turn left an a bridleway down through woodland, heading west. Look out for a footpath sign, then turn sharp right, uphill and in a north-easterly direction.

You come out at the RSPB Nature Reserve, where lunches and teas are served to the public. Beyond, on the same north-east path, is Wiggonholt Church. Retrace your steps to the RSPB reserve then find the path by which you arrived. Return down this path, but instead of re-

Wiggonholt church

turning to the car park, carry on west through Wiggonholt Common. You reach a junction of tarmac roads. Take the one opposite and continue west for over 1 mile to return to Rackham.

Walk 36: Tortington and Binsted

Leave the car at home and use the train to reach our starting point.

Starting Point: Ford Railway Station GR 003049. Map: OS Explorer 121.

Distance: 5 – 6 miles

Terrain: Flat

Local Information: Ford Station is on the Portsmouth to Brighton line.

The Churches

Tortington, St Mary Magdalene: This church is now cared for by the Redundant Churches Fund. In 1847, in *A Day At Arundel*, George Hillier wrote, 'Tortington Church retires a little from the road, but is worthy of a visit, for it has a fine Norman arched doorway, as well as another arch-

way composed of a moulding of grotesque heads of birds and beasts, dividing the nave from the chancel, and a singularly ornamental font. The building itself is completely embossed in a belt of exceedingly rich and luxuriant foliage, sheltering that sequestered spot where the rude forefathers of the hamlet sleep. Where the present and the past are strangely interwoven. Where he who died yesterday reposes by the side of him who died centuries before. Where all is silence

Tortington church

and dust: where comes serious meditation; and where the conscience will be heard.'

Binsted church

Binsted, St Mary: The monks of Tortington Priory built Binsted Church in about 1100. The original Norman walls and three round-headed windows bear witness to their labours. The font with carved arcading is also Norman. There is no arch between nave and chancel. In the splay of the window of the chancel is a 12th-century wall painting of St Margaret of Scotland on the right and the Tree of Life on the left. No other painting of Queen Margaret is known to exist.

The Walk

From Ford Station, walk north along the main road towards Arundel for a short distance. At a sign to Tortington, turn left up to Manor Farm. Follow the fingerpost pointing between farm buildings and the mellow brick house. You step back 900 years. Normans built this neat little church at the southern end of the grounds of Tortington Augustinian Priory. Little remains of the priory today, and when we walk behind the church through iron gates, we are in the garden of New England College. Our walk will take us in the steps of monks and, more recently, students.

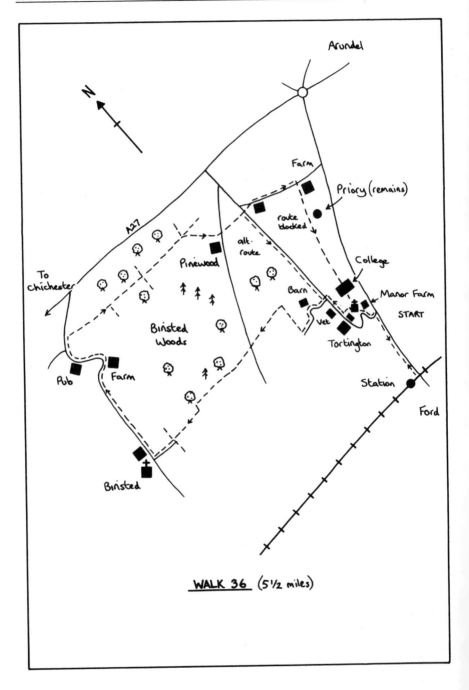

WALK 36 (5½ miles)

Before you push far into the garden, look for a finger post hidden in trees. Trees and hedges give way to lawn, and the stately white house comes into view. The path does not approach the house but turns left into the lane, passing a large, neglected pond on the left. At the lane turn right, walk past the college on the right and then a veterinary hospital on the left. In 200 metres, turn left at a farm track. Follow the track as it curves right and left, past a barn. In 150 metres, turn sharp right into a field.

Here the footpath is less well defined but hugs the hedge on the right. At the corner, cross a footbridge into a small copse. From here continue north across an open field to Binsted Woods. Keep to the path in the woods until you come to a T-junction. Turn left and walk through mixed woodland: oak, sweet chestnut and holly. Cross a narrow lane diagonally and continue west, ignoring paths to left and right. In half a mile you come out of the woodland and still go west. Go round the edge of a small field and find a wide gap in the copse opposite. Fields are in sight through the gap. Cross them with the hedge on the left. In half a mile, if you keep straight on and ignore finger posts, you reach Binsted Lane and the church is facing you.

After visiting Binsted Church, turn north up the lane, passing Church Farm on the right on a bend and the pub just around the bend. Further up Binsted Lane, there is a road junction with Arundel indicated ahead. Follow this way, and after a few metres turn right into a field. Binsted Woods are ahead. Keep heading east through the woods. The ground may be muddy in places with some wooden footbridges crossing the worst parts. Take the third footpath to the right after a clearing. Head south-east through trees, including pines, to a lane with the house called Pinewoods on the right. Cross the lane diagonally left and continue through larch trees to a small stream. Cross the stream and the lane back to Tortington is 150 metres ahead. The site of Tortington Priory is at Priory Farm, nearly half a mile straight on. Otherwise, turn right and walk back to Tortington Church, about 1 mile up the lane.

Walk 37: Ford, Climping and Yapton

Again you may wish to arrive by train, particularly if you decide to extend the walk by 4 miles in order to visit Yapton Church. Let the train take the strain on your journey home!

Starting Point: Ford Railway Station GR 002043. Map: OS Explorer 121.

Distance: 7 miles (with optional 4 miles)

Terrain: Flat

The Churches

Ford, St Andrew: the position of this church, in a small field near the River Arun, is a clue to its past, but few realise that the 900-year-old church is all that remains of a medieval settlement. The manor house, cottages and folk have gone. The dome of the church is still painted white, still to be seen from the nearby River Arun. In medieval times the river was a major highway. It brought flints from the Downs and Caen stone from France. Both were used to build the church. Local rubble was also used for infill. The first church here would have been a stone cross. Some Saxon work can still be seen in the north and west walls. Two small windows in the north wall are Saxon, and two larger ones date from 1200. The south aisle was also added in 1200. The chancel is

Ford church

Norman with a Norman window in the south wall. The other window is a plain lancet of 1250. The three-light east window is one of the best preserved in Decorated style in England. The plain Norman chancel arch is also fine. There was a fire here in 1420, after which the south wall and nave roof were rebuilt. The porch was added in 1640 and has a Dutch gable. As you enter the church, near the door on your right is a wall painting of Doom. Devils drive the damned into the jaws of Hell!

The Chapel at Bailiffscourt, Atherington, near Climping: In the grounds of a hotel, Bailiffscourt is a Norman chapel. Phone Littlehampton 01903 723511 for permission to visit the chapel. It stands a little apart from the other medieval buildings which were imported early this century by Lord Moyne. The chapel, which had been neglected, was restored and allowed to stand in its natural beauty. It has a fine trefoil east window of 13th-century design. Soon after the Norman Conquest, the manor close to the sea was given to St Martin's Abbey of Seez in Normandy. For 300 years or more a monk was bailiff here and appointed lay brothers to help him They worshipped in this chapel. The estate became known as Bailiffscourt.

Clymping, St Mary: Rising above Ford Prison and nearby suburban houses is the 40ft tower of Clymping Church. It was built in 1170 as a watchtower, to stop unwelcome boats from the Channel sailing up the River Arun to the important port of Arundel. Clymping itself was a sizeable manor. In 1102, Savaric Fitzcane took it over from the Montgomeries of Arundel. For 400 years, the lords of the manor of Ford and Clymping were descendants of Savaric. The tower is late Norman with complex stone ornament, but the elaborate west door, with bold dogtooth and zigzag carvings is the focal point. There is a trefoil head to the doorway with round arches above and twisted columns on either side. This work and that of the window above is unique and perfect. In 1230 a pure Early English church was built next to the tower. Caen stone has been skilfully worked throughout. No doubt the flat-bottomed boats which brought Caen stone from Normandy were welcome.

Yapton, St Mary the Virgin: In contrast with the concrete sheds and industrial roads of Ford Airport, the church stands in a picturesque corner of the village of Yapton. Built without today's precision tools, the church is a fortunate, unspoilt survivor. The 14th-century timber and plaster west porch appears to lean one way. The Transition-Norman tower definitely leans; it is 11 degrees out! Thick buttresses, which generations of villagers have added to prop the tower, are still in place. A 'Sussex Cap', a pyramid of timber and a cross complete the tower. The nave was built at the same time as the tower, between 1180 and 1230. The chancel and arch are Early English. There is a round Saxon font.

The Walk

From Ford Station, walk across the level crossing and south on the pavement. Pass a caravan site on the left and the path to Ford Church is on the left, opposite the road to Yapton. As you approach the church you pass Lock Cottage on the left. Apply here for the key to the church.

After Ford Church, turn right and continue on the path north-east to the River Arun. Turn right here on the river bank, towards Littlehampton. Pass Ford Prison and nature reserve and then a small sewage works, all on the right. In 1½ miles the footpath passes under the A259 Bognor to Littlehampton road. This brings you to Littlehampton Marina where coffee is served on-board ship, the *Sea Horse,* or tea can be had at a nearby café. Refreshed, carry on to the entrance to the marina and pass the drawbridge on your left. Cross to the road opposite, towards the golf course. At the entrance of the car park, turn right into a footpath which follows the northern edge of the golf course for over half a mile.

At a cross-paths turn left, pass the mill on your right and keep going to the sea. At the shore turn right and walk along the beach for half a mile. Some marine plants, sea holly and sea kale grow here. At Climping car park turn right and follow the road north. Bailiffscourt Hotel is on the left. In the grounds, amongst other ancient buildings, is a single-cell Saxon chapel.

Opposite the entrance to Bailiffscourt is a footpath across flat, treeless farmland towards Littlehampton. Follow it for a short way then turn left up a wide track to Climping Village School. Turn right here then left past the thatched cottages of Amberley Hotel. At the roundabout on the A259, cross to the road opposite Church Lane. This passes through Climping to Ford. Walk along the pavement and in under half a mile, Climping Church can be seen on your right. This same pavement will take you back to Ford Station in 1 mile.

For the optional detour to Yapton Church: *In places, this route follows busy roads.* From Climping Church, cross Church Lane to the footpath opposite. Go over a small field, past a barn and to a concrete road. This serves the storage sheds of industrial units, a 20th-century concrete jungle. Head for Roll Call cafe. From here climb into Ford Airport, now used as a drive-in Sunday market. Head north-west towards a housing estate. Here, turn left towards Yapton Road, served by a pavement. Turn right along the pavement to the centre of Yapton. Cross the village green to the church. From Yapton Church, go to the end of the wall in Church Lane for a well-hidden path to the right. This emerges at crosspaths. Turn right and head for a farm hut which you pass on your left. There are views to the Downs. Follow the path and turn left at finger posts. At Ford Lane, turn right, keeping to the edge of the road back to Ford.

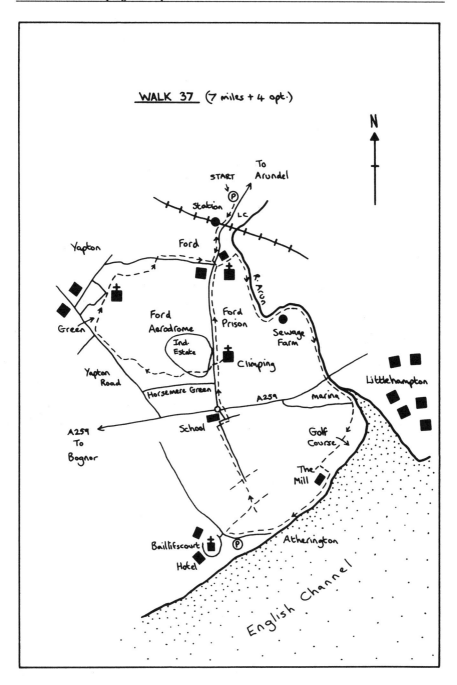

Walk 38: Eartham, Slindon and Madehurst

Here is a fairly short, circular walk to the interesting village of Slindon – a very pleasant way to spend an afternoon. But, if you have the time, a much better idea is to begin in the morning, spend time in Slindon, and then tackle the 7 miles to Madehurst and back to Eartham.

Starting Point: Eartham playing fields, on the road to Bognor. GR 940094. Map: OS Explorer 121.

Distance: 4 miles to Slindon and back. 11 miles to Slindon and Madehurst and back to Eartham. (The longer route continues from opposite Slindon College GR 960085.)

Terrain: Hilly

The Churches

Eartham, St Margaret: Described in Petworth, Walk 9.

Slindon, St Richard: This Catholic church was built in 1865 by C.A. Buckler. When open, you may be fortunate – as I was – to hear beautiful recorded music pervading this lofty church.

Slindon, St Mary: This is the parish church. It has undergone many changes over the years. St Wilfrid gave Slindon to Canterbury and there was an archbishop's palace where Slindon House is now. The original chancel and nave of a small, simple church have disappeared, apart from a little window in the north of the nave and a square Norman font. The chancel and nave were rebuilt in the 13th century. A west tower, north aisle, bay and south aisle have been added. In the 15th century, arches were made in each wall of the nave. There is a fine 16th-century effigy of a knight in armour. In 1866, the church was heavily restored.

Madehurst, St Mary: The church is tucked away between cottages at the southern end of Madehurst. Entry to the church is through the thick-buttressed tower and a 13th-century pointed arch. Remains of the Norman origins of the church can be found in the small round-headed doorway in the nave. The church was restored and enlarged in 1864. The population of Madehurst could not have been much greater then, so why such a big church?

The Walk

From Eartham, take the footpath east across the playing field. On your right are fine views over Slindon Woods and fields to the sea. The path zigzags up to Nore Hill. At the T-junction turn right down a tree-lined track until, in just over half a mile, you reach a tarmac lane. Cross diagonally to woods and enter Slindon Park. Follow the narrow path through woodland until you reach the main track, where you turn left up to the National Trust Centre. Here the track curves left back to the road. Turn right up a path beside the road to the village. The village of Slindon is managed by the National Trust. You pass Slindon College on your right and the flint Catholic church on your left. At a crossroads with a tree and seat in the centre, turn right. The Anglican church is 50 metres down on the right.

You may wish to explore more of this interesting village before you go back to Slindon College and either returning to Eartham or extending the walk to Madehurst.

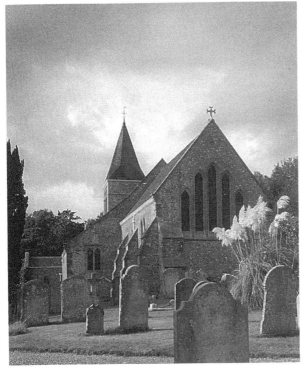

Silndon, St Mary

To return to Eartham: Go past Slindon College and follow the road as it curves away from the village. Turn sharp right down a lane and Slindon Folly can be seen on the hill ahead. Turn left at Courthill Farm and follow the wide track, ignoring right-hand paths (except to visit the folly if you feel so inclined). When you reach the T-junction, turn right and retrace your steps up the tree-lined track. Look out for a stile in the hedge on your left

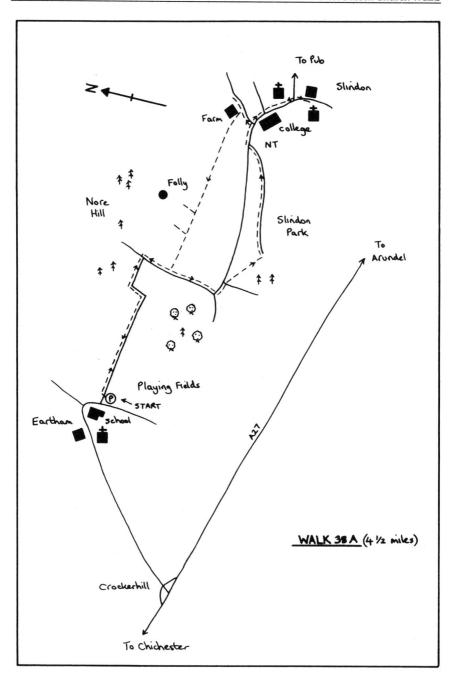

N

To Pub

Slindon

Farm

college

NT

Folly

Nore
Hill

Slindon
Park

To
Arundel

A27

Playing Fields

P ← START

Eartham

school

WALK 38 A (4 ½ miles)

Crockerhill

To Chichester

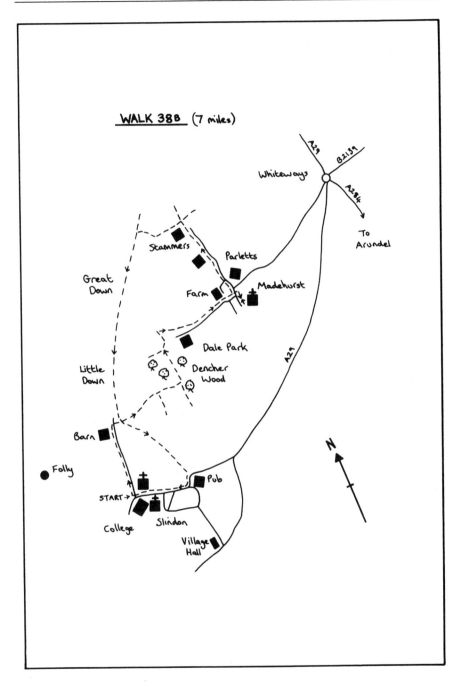

and return to the playing fields. Keep straight on when you reach the village road then turn left for Eartham Church.

To walk from Slindon to Madehurst: Follow the woodland track opposite Slindon College. This leads north, uphill, with glimpses of Slindon Folly on a hill to the left. After a barn on the left, look for a chalky slope in a gap in the trees on the right. Go through to a grassy meeting place of footpaths, supplied with a seat. To the north-east a white building in wooded hills is Dale Park House. Bignor Hill is more to the north. Due east, your footpath is facing you. Follow it down a slope. The edge of a field is on your left and woodland on your right. Ignore all paths to the right and, at a T-junction, turn left on to a good, firm track through the trees, including yews, of Dencher Wood. At a cross-paths you emerge into Dale Park. Turn right and cross diagonally north-east up a sloping field to a farm gate, and then into the grounds of Dale Park House, now hidden by trees. Turn left on to a stony track through trees. At a private tarmac road, turn right downhill. Eventually, you pass a field on the left with cedar trees and go down towards New Barn Farm. Before you reach the farm at a crosspaths, there is a track sharp right through flat parkland – go straight on, heading east up to Madehurst. At a tarmac lane turn right, round a bend and the church is on the left.

To return to Slindon from Madehurst Church: Retrace your steps but do not go down to New Barn Farm. Instead, follow the tarmac lane north and take the first turning left, another tarmac lane. Turn right past Parletts Farm; the lane zigzags before straightening. In 1 mile pass remote Stammers Cottage. The Downs are ahead and no cars are allowed. At a cross-paths turn left and west along a path which hugs the northern edge of Stammers Wood. It then dips into a little secret valley and rises steeply to a downland field. It turns sharp right here then left and enters storm-damaged woodland. At the T-junction, turn left through scrub which opens onto Great Down, with magnificent views to the coast. Halnaker Windmill is to the right. Our path leads south, downhill for about 1 mile with views all the way. At the original grassy meeting place of footpaths, keep straight on to a track south up to open fields and into Mill Lane, Slindon. Keep south, and at the T-junction of village lanes turn left for the pub or turn right for Slindon College.

Walk 39: Sompting and Coombes

This walk starts approximately 10 miles east of Arundel on the A27.

Starting Point: Sompting Church car park, north of the A27, GR 162057. Maps: OS Explorers 121 & 122 or Landranger 198.

Distance: 7 miles

Terrain: Hilly

Local Information: The nearest stations are East Worthing and Lancing.

Sompting church

The Churches

Sompting Church: The church stands almost alone in the rising Downs. The village or conurbation of Sompting is south across the A27. The church tower, with stone pilaster strips on each wall, is a monument to Saxon architecture. The spire or Rhenish helm is the only one in England. There are others in West Germany, and this spire gives evidence of pre-Conquest links. Small Saxon windows are high in the tower. Inside are original timbers, and there is a fine Saxon tower arch. You enter the church through the south porch and realise immediately that here is a huge, historic shrine. Knights Templar built the south transept as a private chapel in 1180. It is spacious and solid, a church in its own right. The north transept is also a church with chapels for the Templars. The 12th century nave and chancel are on the site of the original church mentioned in Domesday in 1086. It has no chancel arch. In 1324 the Knights of St John or the Hospitaller took over the church. We owe St John's Ambulance to them.

Coombes Church: Almost part of the Downs, where it has lain for over 900 years. It was once the centre of the medieval village of Cumbe. Little remains of the village, but the villagers have left their message on the walls of the church. There are 12th-century pious paintings: scenes from the Nativity on north and south walls and Christ in Majesty above the chancel arch. There is a humourous painting on the side of the chancel arch: a man grimacing as he bends under the weight of masonry. Changes have been made to the church over the ages. The Saxon nave has been widened. Windows in the nave were altered in 14th century. The chancel was enlarged at the same time and the walls aligned with those of the nave to form a rectangular building. The south doorway and chancel arch (2ft 6ins thick) remain intact from the early Norman church. Between the two 15th-century windows south in the chancel is an 11th-century door. The porch and east window are 16th century. Horsham slabs are on the roof. The bellcote is 18th century.

Coombes church

The Walk

Just below Sompting Church car park, follow the path west with views over Worthing to the sea on the left. In less than half a mile you come to a T-junction. Turn right up a concrete farm track which emerges on the Downs and becomes a grassy path. Over to the left, is Lychpole Hill. Our path turns right up to the farm cottages of Beggars Bush. Continue past the cottages to the road, turn left and continue uphill for half a mile to a parking space where a footpath crosses the road.

Turn right up the footpath, heading east. Ignore all paths right and left. In a quarter of a mile, keep to the left of a pylon and walk straight on over open downland for one mile. To the left is Annington Hill and there is a fine view along Winding Bottom to Steyning. You are high on Coombe Head and the River Ador and cement works are ahead. The path veers right towards the hamlet of Coombes. First to be noticed is the farm, and it is tempting to follow the farm track down the hill. Instead, keep to the footpath, following the direction of the fingerpost. The footpath is at the top edge of the field and passes the church below on the left. Go through the farm gate and turn immediately left down a narrow, steep path lost in woodland. This brings you to the delightful little church. There is a campsite and barn below. The River Adur is beyond, but the view is marred by cement works on the other side.

Return up the wooded path back to the Downs. Face the farm gate but do not go through it. Turn left and head south over fields (there is a view to the left of the imposing Lancing Chapel and College). Go down to Cow Bottom, an animal enclosure, and up Lancing Hill. Keep south to sculptured Downs behind North Lancing. There are wide views to the sea and it is even possible to make out gleaming white cliffs to the east: these are the Seven Sisters beyond Seaford.

At a T-junction of paths turn right and climb the north-west edge of sparse woodland for nearly a mile – Lancing Ring nature reserve on your left. All paths to the left lead to Lancing. Ignore these until open downland, wher the paths curve round and over the slopes ahead. Turn left then immediately right to continue north-west on a path which runs parallel to the one you have just left. This leads down to a sunken track which curves west around Cross Dyke. There is a high wire fence on the left at first. After half a mile leave the fence behind and head south-west on a more open track. This leads down to a T-junction with a farm track. From here: **either** continue down the track to the A27, where there is a path on the right to Sompting; **otherwise,** turn left down the farm track until you come to a path off to the right. This brings you out at Titch Hill Farm on the Sompting Road. Turn left and go down past a wooded hill on the right as you curve back to Sompting Church.

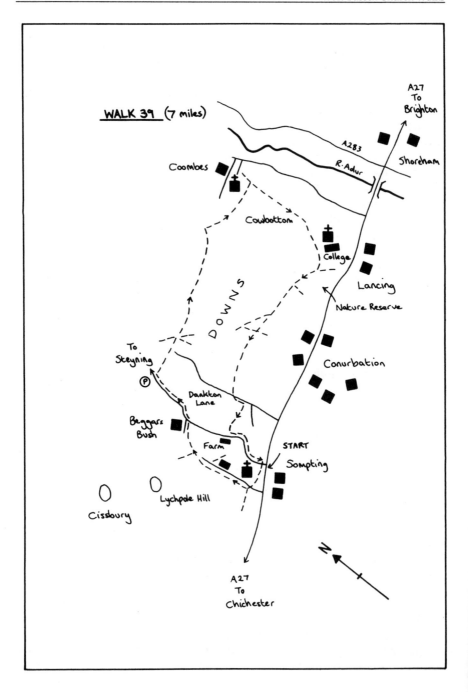

WALK 39 (7 miles)

A27
To
Brighton

Shoreham

A283

R. Adur

Coombes

Cowbottom

D O W N S

College

Lancing

Nature Reserve

To
Steyning

P

Dankton
Lane

Conurbation

Beggars
Bush

Farm

START

Sompting

Cissbury

Lychpole Hill

N

A27
To
Chichester

Walk 40: Washington Common, Sullington and Washington

This walk starts about 12 miles from Arundel. It can be reached by car via Amberley and Storrington.

Starting Point: National Trust car park, north of the A283, Storrington to Washington road and half a mile up George's Lane. GR 115141. Map: OS Explorer 121.

Distance: 5 – 6 miles

Terrain: Hilly

The Churches

Sullington Church: A church of perfect simplicity. The nave is narrow, suggesting Saxon proportions. At the base of the tower, Saxon stones are set 'long and short'. Apart from this the tower is Norman. The main body of the church is Early English, with the exception of the Decorated east window with its network of tracery. The 'Mary' window is more recent. The north aisle was once a chantry, founded by Richard, Earl of Arundel in 1389. Near the entrance to the church, which is through the tower, lies a knight skilfully carved in marble. This little corner of Sussex, church, farm, manor and tithe barn, is not quite idyllic. A farming industry is here and corrugated buildings jostle the church as tractors turn in the yard.

Washington, St Mary: The church stands on a hill on the site of a tiny Norman church. The first recorded vicar is Bovo in 1174. The early church was linked to the Priory of Sale at Beeding. Transport to and from Sale was on foot or horse. Never could they have foreseen the speeding traffic of the A24, now below the church. A narrow bridge links the church with the Downs. Knights Templar built a larger church with a tower. Later the tower was incorporated as a lean-to to a new Tudor tower. In 1865 the church was again dismantled and rebuilt. Only the tower was spared.

The Walk

From Washington Common National Trust car park, walk back down George's Lane. You are heading south and the Downs in front are beck-

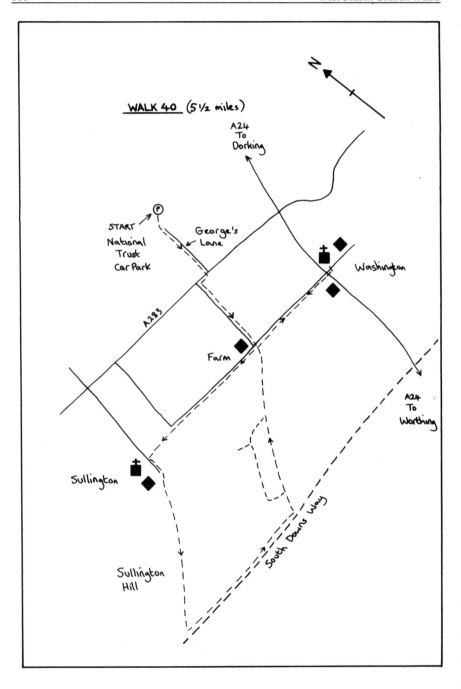

oning. Do not let them distract; you need all your wits to cross the A283. Diagonally opposite is a farm track and footpath on a private road to Rowdell, still heading south. After cottages, turn right across fields. Keep a westerly direction for 1 mile, to Sullington Church.

After you have seen the church, now is your chance to climb up into the Downs. The footpath is just where you would expect it: on the track south from the church. After 100 metres you have a choice of paths, each leading to the South Downs Way. The right-hand one is prettier; the left-hand track is shorter. Once on top, admire the view! We shall not be here for long unless you have brought a picnic.

Turn left and walk along the South Downs Way for 1 mile. At the first turning, a sign 'SDW Route Avoiding Dangerous Road'. Turn left down to the fields. Only this time when you reach the cross-paths, turn right, eastwards to Washington. There is a footpath over the A24 which enables you to cross to the village in safety. The church is the first building you see as you cross. The village is ahead, descending the hill to the pub at the bottom!

From Washington Church, retrace your steps back over the bridge and along the path which brought you here. Once back at the cottages, Rowdell (our third visit), turn right and you are heading north along the same farm track to the A283 and the diagonal crossing to George's Lane.

Sullington church

Bibliography

A History of Sussex J.R. Armstrong (Philimore)

Off The Beaten Track in Sussex Arthur S. Cooke (Herbert Jenkins Ltd, 3 Yorke St, London, SW1)

English Life, To The End of the Middle Ages J.D. Griffith Davies (Alfred Knopf Ltd, Frome, Somerset)

The Victorian Churches of Sussex D. Robert Elleray (Phillimore)

Notes on Sussex Churches Harrison Hove

The Buildings of England – Sussex Nairn and N. Pevsner (Harmondsworth)

Twelfth Century Church Architecture in Sussex Richard Roberts (The Book Guild)

Coldwaltham, A Story of Three Hamlets Sandra Saer (SMH Enterprises, Pear Tree Cottage, Watersfield, West Sussex, RH20 1NG)

The Lost Villages of Sussex John Vigar (Dovecote Press)

Ancient Churches of Sussex Ken and Joyce Roedale (Whiteman)

The Architecture of Britain Doreen Yarwood (B.T. Batsford)